A Penguin Special
Who Cares?

Penelope Leach was educated at Cambridge University, where she read History, and at the London School of Economics, where she obtained a Social Work Diploma and then a Ph.D. in Social Psychology. She has researched into juvenile crime for the Home Office and into the development and upbringing of children for the Medical Research Council. She has contributed extensively to the *Sunday Times* and *The Times*, and to *Mother and Baby*, *Mother* and other magazines. Her frequent broadcasting has included a major series on children in local authority care for B.B.C. further education, as well as series for 'Woman's Hour' and many phone-in programmes. She is a Vice-President of the Pre-School Playgroups Association, a member of the Committee of the Developmental Section of the British Psychological Society, and a sponsor of the Society of Teachers Opposed to Corporal Punishment. She is also outside medical editor for Penguin Books. Her first book, *Babyhood*, was published in Penguins and her second, *Baby and Child*, already published in fifteen countries, will soon be published by Penguin.

Penelope Leach is married to an energy specialist. They have two children, a girl and a boy.

Penelope Leach

Who Cares?

A New Deal for Mothers and Their Small Children

PENGUIN BOOKS

Penguin Books Ltd, Harmondsworth,
Middlesex, England
Penguin Books, 625 Madison Avenue,
New York, New York 10022, U.S.A.
Penguin Books Australia Ltd, Ringwood,
Victoria, Australia
Penguin Books Canada Ltd, 2801 John Street,
Markham, Ontario, Canada L3R 1B4
Penguin Books (N.Z.) Ltd, 182–190 Wairau Road,
Auckland 10, New Zealand

First published 1979

Set, printed and bound in Great Britain by
Cox & Wyman Ltd, London, Reading and Fakenham
Set in Intertype Times

*To the Pre-School Playgroups Association
which* does *care and to my friends within it
who asked: 'What about the under-threes?'*

Contents

1. The Family Bandwagon

Everyone is for the family. Concern for it transcends traditional barriers between political parties, social classes and sexes. The statements and demands made by spokespeople fill the columns of our newspapers and give rise to my new party game: Happy Families 1979.

'Any government must be profoundly concerned with the present fragmentation of family life, because of all the social ills that flow from it . . .'

'Our government is putting together a national family policy to strengthen the stability and the quality of family life in Britain . . .'

Take away the quotation marks and those two quotes could run on as one. But the first is from Patrick Jenkin, Tory spokesman on family policy, while the second is from James Callaghan, Labour Prime Minister. That is the game: find matching remarks on the family made by traditional opponents and then see if your friends can tell who said what. You will find that you can play it not only with the words of politicians but with the CBI and the TUC and with men and women too. The family is a vital institution, they say. All men of goodwill should put its needs to the forefront of their thinking. The family needs more support, more professional help, more educators, more care-takers, more institutions. It needs tax reforms and free school milk; child-care facilities and secure accommodation for juvenile offenders; reform of divorce law and less pornography. The family needs counselling and it needs money. State money to show state concern.

Arch-enemies do not like to sound the same as each other, so you can play an interesting variation on the game by seeking out their objections. David Ennals, Secretary of State for Health and Social Security and the Labour spokesman on family policy, maintains that he can see a clear 'difference of philosophy' between his own party and the Tories. Patrick Jenkin makes it into an open competition with the words: 'But we got there first! Mr Callaghan claims to have discovered the family this year, but I don't think he carries conviction.'

I do not think that any of them carry conviction, nor do I think that this tide of concern for 'the family' is as benevolent as it is intended to appear. Families, whatever form they take, are the most basic form of social grouping for individual human beings; but it is not as human beings that their members are being seen. Rather they are producer-consumers and the families they make up are the basic production-consumption units of an acquisitive society dedicated to the preservation of a growth economy. Cut through the cackle of concern and that is the core. Money, not happiness, well-being or anything else you like to call it, is the central issue for politicians, employers' organizations, trades unions and other opinion leaders. For them, people are defined by the jobs they do for money and if their happiness is considered at all it is assumed to equate with what they can earn and therefore buy. A good government – or one which can hope to stay in power – is one which keeps industry rolling along with jobs and wages for all and prices held in line. A good welfare system is one which supports those who, through no fault of their own, earn less than most people, but which also puts heavy pressure on those who could earn more for themselves if they tried. A good education is one which prepares people to get ahead within the work-ethic and which disgorges them clasping pieces of paper which will prove to employers that it is producing employables. Problems, however personal they may feel to the sufferer, are ultimately caused, ameliorated or cured by private or public finance. And where public money is actually handed out to solve problems, it is used to prime the family, or the company, money-making pump, so that individuals can rejoin the rat-race of earning for themselves or companies can return a profit-balance.

The Confederation of British Industry is currently leading a study commission on the family. It is an employers' organization so we must expect its eventual findings to be slanted towards families-for-industry rather than industry-for-families. But the Trades Union Congress which represents the members of those families has just published a report and *its* recommendations are slanted that way too. Although it represents people and would describe itself as being 'for the people', its suggestions are for workers. The report is built on the assumption that everyone wants to work, everyone has a right to work, everyone's self-respect is dependent upon work. Obstacles to people working must be removed. If those obstacles happen to be people too, whether very old or very young ones, they should be gathered into groups out of the worker's way and there, in institutions, their care can constitute that vital job of work for somebody else.

Any society is made up of people and meant to be for them. I find ours increasingly ugly because it puts what people produce above what they are and in doing so it removes any room to manoeuvre for kinds of happiness or creative activity which may have more to do with relationships than with material wealth. No society can survive without children and, in this sense, they must be its most important product. But new human beings are seen as a slow-maturing capital investment which must not be allowed to interfere with what is currently profitable. The people of the future must not be allowed to hamper the workers of today.

I am angry on behalf of all babies and small children in our society because I see the needs of more and more of them being less and less well-met. I am angry on behalf of their mothers because I see society making it increasingly difficult for them to recognize and meet those needs. And I am angry on behalf of father-partners too, because society demands of them a kind of caring and cooperation which it simultaneously prevents them from giving. So like everybody else I am concerned for families, but my concern is out of step with the current trend; I think we have got our priorities wrong.

Families Are People

Some form of family meets a basic human need for relationships with other people who care. Despite bitter revilement by some and interesting experiments in alternative ways of living by others, nobody, either in Britain or elsewhere, has yet come up with a long-term alternative that works. Human beings are not solely individuals, choosing if and when they will form partnerships or groupings with other individuals. Very few of us want, or can manage, to live for long entirely alone in the sense of taking full responsibility for ourselves and our happiness, separate from everybody else. Even the most independent person can become ill – physically or mentally – and will, from time to time, become lonely, miserable and purposeless. When that happens he or she will seek other human beings. Like elephants, we are group creatures and, condemned to aloneness, we too turn into rogues.

As fast as people leave their parents and whatever extended family was associated with life in their home, they seek new groupings. For very young adults, shared flats, houses and digs provide some of the security of family. For those who live alone, office, factory or college friendships can give some feeling of having a place in a group. Where even this is missing, the single bedsitter is among urban civilization's loneliest dwelling-places and the search for 'somebody of my own' can become desperate. Many of the young people who profess to have hated – or at least to have become quite different from – their parents and the communities in which they were reared, rush straight into their re-creation to escape the exposure of solitude. Others involve themselves in groups whose activities they may neither truly enjoy nor even approve of, because it is better to be part of the gang, the commune or the new religion than to be part of nothing. Some of the girls who become pregnant, perhaps out of relationships entered to combat aloneness, refuse the abortions suggested to them by well-meaning counsellors. Few of them truly want to have and rear this particular baby. But the role of single mother is at least a recognized one and anything, even a baby, seems better than being quite alone again.

Not every relationship entered into on the basis of 'anybody is better than nobody' produces a child. But many become consolidated, perhaps turned into marriages, on the basis, conscious or unconscious, of being better than nothing. Cynical? Perhaps, but it is rare, at any stage in adult life, for a partner to leave without another to go to. With exceptions among the peculiarly self-sufficient on the one hand and the peculiarly ill-treated on the other, the pattern of our escalating divorce rate is that one partner leaves for somebody else so that the one who is alone has not left but been abandoned.

Families are important because they provide people both with a sense of personal identity and with other people whose basic concern can be taken for granted. Curiously enough both those two hold good even when relationships within an individual family are strained to the limits of television drama. Angry people can only reject the identity given them by their family of origin, *if they know what it is.* If they want to be 'different' they need something to be different from. At the same time people can only have real humdinger family rows if the relationships contain concern. We do not scream at strangers for their personal life-styles; we ignore them. Screaming means concern and being ignored is what human beings can bear least equably.

Unfortunately, clear though we may be that 'family' is important, we suffer considerable confusion about what it actually *is.* Biological definitions would seem to make the matter clear enough. Blood relationships give rise to everything from the obvious mother or grandfather to those complex and sometimes incomprehensible relationships like second-cousin-twice-removed. But even biological definitions of family have to allow for the new blood called into the 'line' by family-members mating. Traditionally, all acknowledged sexual relationships were marriages and gave rise to relationships-in-law. Nowadays most of us have lovers-out-of-law either instead of, or at least until, we acquire brothers-in-law. If your sister sets up a long-term relationship with a man she does not marry, is he a member of your family and is she a member of his? If the pair of them have a child, that gives you a niece or nephew but does it make the father an uncle to your own children? Or was he that already by virtue of going to bed with their aunt? Is a widowed or divorced woman's permanent, living-in lover the stepfather of her existing children? Are your children cousins to the children of their aunt's lover by somebody else?

A dinner-party game, perhaps, but an important one. That family tradition had to do with the linking of blood lines through marriage but it also had to do with the acceptance of responsibilities. If you married somebody, you knew you were stuck with a mother-in-law. A marriage ceremony or the acquisition of a legal certificate may genuinely make no difference to the couple concerned, neither making their relationship more or less secure or likely to last. But the absence of it or its cancellation through divorce, means that people have to work out their *extended* family responsibilities for themselves. A ten-year-old boy, worried by a series of family fatalities, recently worked on this. He had a perfectly healthy pair of parents of his own I am glad to say, but he also had an aunt who had recently divorced the husband whom he had known since birth, and was now living with a newcomer. 'If all of you and all my own people died, would Jack look after me or would Joseph come back and be my family?' Pertinent if unanswerable. Then there was an elderly man who badly missed his Saturday evenings in the pub with his son-in-law and protested bitterly that 'he hasn't divorced *me* you know'. There is even a flat nearby which contains four youngsters, mingled sons and daughters of a widower who set up house with an unmarried mother, lived with her for ten years and then agreed to part. 'They made us a family and we hated each other. Then they unmade it again and they expected us to split. No way.'

The whole concept of family as a mutually-caring, mutually-supportive, mutually-responsible group runs counter to current trends. People are supposed to have their minds and their aspirations on their jobs, not on each other. They are supposed to find freedom and personal fulfilment in a get-up-and-go philosophy which takes them, in advertisements, to 'a new life of adventure in sunny Australia', or in reality to another factory in a new dormitory area. Objections about 'leaving mother behind' cut no ice with authority and draw derision from peers. Society encourages a tendency, which often seems lemming-like in its disaster-potential, to move, geographically, whenever a crisis point is reached personally. Young people leave school and as if the transition to work, college or the dole were not crisis enough, they are expected to 'leave home' simultaneously. People get married and are expected to search for, if not to find, 'homes of their own'. They have babies and, just when family and familiar neighbours could be of maximum practical as well as emotional support, they range afield for 'a bigger place'. People reach retirement and go off to a bungalow elsewhere. A partner leaves or dies and the one who is left is encouraged to 'start afresh'. Planning and housing policies both reflect and redouble this disruption of family-within-community. Look, for example, at some of the most effective methods of getting yourself up a local authority housing list: get yourself thrown out by your parents; have a baby or, better yet, two or three babies; accept a job with a firm which is 'moving out'; volunteer to vacate your home in exchange for a smaller one elsewhere for retirement...

So we all move about, punctuating our lives with changes of place and loss of people and the reality of 'family' in Britain today ends up as two adults responsible for one or more small children. We call that set-up a 'nuclear family' and thus make it sound more serious and sociological. But there are few kinds of nuclei which can function satisfactorily in isolation from whatever they are the nuclei *of*. Nuclear families are no exception to this general biological rule. When the concept of the nuclear family is further stretched to include the euphemistically entitled 'single-parent family', the whole idea of 'family' becomes as absurd a basis for the organization of society as it is a ridiculously inadequate relationship network. Yet it is these isolated breeding couples and their offspring who all those politicians and opinion leaders refer to when they talk of 'the family'. And it is with them and with society's distorted view of them and above all of their children, that I am concerned here.

Nuclear Families and Pre-school Children

I am going to argue that meeting the needs of babies and small children is important and that doing so in a nuclear family today is extremely difficult. I am going to try to show that the public concern expressed for these families is largely phoney and that the help offered to them is unhelpful. After all that, I shall try to set out the real needs of young families, as I understand them, and to suggest both long-term educational methods and immediate practical means by which these needs could be met without postulating revolution or a new society.

But before I embark, there is one widespread misconception which must be put right. It was expressed to me over and over again at a meeting I attended last week and it goes like this:

All mothers work nowadays . . .
Now that everybody works, it's different . . .
It's no good talking about babies being better off with their mums because their mums are out at work, you know. You're out of date.

I may be out of date in many ways, but those speakers had their facts wrong. The great majority of children under five in Britain today are cared for in their own homes by their own mothers. I will come, shortly, to the questions of whether they should be so, whether the mothers want it that way and so forth. But right now I am concerned only with the fact that, however it may be made to appear by the authorities, public figures and the media, *most mothers with children under five do not go out to work.*

16

Taking the last available statistics from the Office of Population Censuses with the Central Statistical Office, there are *three million* children under five whose mothers look after them full-time at home. In contrast there are *850,000* children in this age-group whose mothers undertake some paid employment outside their homes. Of those, 306,000 have mothers who work for twelve hours or less each week. 372,000 have mothers who work for more than twelve but less than thirty hours each week, while only 172,000 have mothers who are at work for more than thirty hours weekly.

Not only is the total percentage of mothers minute, the hours worked by the majority of this minute percentage are extremely short, too.

Babies and young children must have care every minute of every day, so the mother who goes out at all must clearly make some arrangements for them to be looked after. But the problems and possible solutions which are relevant to those who are out for such short periods are quite different from those associated with the popular image of the 'working mother'. It is notoriously difficult to establish exactly when and where part-timers work, but anyone who lives in the community, rather than in a statistical office, knows that many of them undertake domestic or office cleaning or relief and rush-period work in shops and other service industries. Some take their children with them; others arrange their hours to fit with time when their partners or older children will be at home; still others make informal arrangements with neighbours to 'mind the baby' during the couple of afternoons that they are absent from home. With hours as short as this, the disruption to both mother and child is usually minimal. The mother's available time for household chores and child-care is still ample. The child's daily life is still lived basically at home and with mother. Indeed the days when father gives him breakfast because mother is doing an early shift, or when he is taken to the neighbour for two or three hours at a time, may be highspots of his week.

On these figures, only about 400,000 children under five have mothers whose outside working-hours amount to the equivalent of five half-days or more each week. Only at that level does the 'working mother' image begin to be appropriate. Unless her hours happen to comprise night-shifts (as is common, for example, in the textile areas of the Midlands), her child will have to pass substantial chunks of daily life somewhere other than home and/or with someone other than parents. And she herself will face some compression of other aspects of her life: routine chores, child-care and leisure, into short hours. But not until we reach that group of 172,000 children whose mothers work for more than thirty hours per week are we really talking about 'working mothers' as most people visualize them.

2. The Official View of Help for Families

Help for families is central to the hustings of the major political parties, documented in the deliberations of endless governmental committees and working parties and a sure-fire applause-inducer for trades union and other speech-makers. Most of it is a con. The help which is proposed or applauded is not based on what is known of children's development and their consequent needs. It is dictated instead by political and economic considerations swathed, for decency and fashionable acceptance, in the banners of the women's movement.

The provisions which are being made, planned or promised 'for' children under five are not for the well-being or the happiness of those children at all. They are for women's votes and women's labour. Instead of using its resources to help families – and especially mothers – *through* the early years of child-care, that amorphous conglomeration which I will label the state seems set on helping them *out*. Instead of devoting thought and the imaginative deployment of scarce money and personnel to making it easier for women to do an excellent job with and for their children, authorities seem clear that the answer to every problem peculiar to being a parent is to take over the child-care from them. If the money and the staff were available to turn every politician's promise or union leader's demand into an actual bricks-and-mortar institution, our streets would be almost as empty of children as are the streets of Moscow during factory hours.

The bitter part of the situation is that this terrifying trend is partly the fault of well-meaning people like me. For years we have complained that the needs of under-fives were neglected by the state. For years we have moaned because voluntary organizations like the Pre-School Playgroups Association, the National Association for the Welfare of Children in Hospital or the National Childbirth Trust did not get sufficient government recognition; for which read grant-aid. We thought that we were working to persuade political and other opinion leaders to take notice of the needs of very young children. But all we seem to have succeeded in doing is to make them take notice of the adults around those children. They plan to give parents – especially female parents – what they think they want. They neither know, nor seem to care, what children need.

In support of this formidable indictment I will cite a recently published report by the Central Policy Review Staff (1978). This document is primarily concerned with services for the young children of working mothers, and as such I shall refer to it later, but its early statements clearly outline the attitudes of the many organizations who gave evidence, towards young families as a whole:

> Most parents with young children need advice and help in caring for them and bringing them up . . .
> Governmental agencies have an increasing role to play in providing the essential health and advisory services to help young parents . . .
> The assumption that *in normal circumstances* (my italics) the family can cope is now no longer a sufficient answer . . .

I suggest that each and every one of these assumptions is questionable especially when it is realized that they refer to all parents and young children in our society. These are not families who have sought help or been discovered to be labouring under special and identifiable difficulties. They are me, you, our friends and neighbours, the people we meet at the shops and around the school gates, in the parks and at the bus stop. Can we really not cope? Do we truly need advice and help in our early child-care? Do we want governmental agencies to have an increasing role? The compilers of this report have an unequivocal answer:

The issue is not, as is frequently supposed, whether the government should be involved at all in so domestic a relationship as that between parents and a pre-school child, where there are no obvious social inadequacies. The real question is whether the government's existing role is sufficient ...

It is widely recognized by the many agencies which gave evidence to this group and by those who reported for the earlier Department of Health and Social Security document 'Preparation for Parenthood' (1974), that young parents used to 'cope' and that they did so with the help of their own extended families. But acknowledgement of the breakdown of this traditional and informal support network is not accompanied by regret, much less by suggestions that its maintenance or reformation would be desirable. Apart from a passing suggestion from the Association of Municipal Corporations that 'attempts should be made in large redevelopment schemes to rehouse young families near their extended families ...' most of the consulting organizations take the end of 'grandparenting' for granted or even applaud it. The National Association for Mental Health, for example, pointed out that: 'In many families the influence of the maternal grandmother on the mother's child-rearing methods and attitudes is considerable ...' but made the point in order to stress that such influence is not always for the good.

Other agencies are aware that grandmothers still exist and can form a valuable corpus of support and help for young families. Yet they take extended family breakdown so much for granted that they suggest that children should benefit from contact with other people's grandparents rather than their own. The County Councils' Association:

The grandparents themselves, however, are still in existence and many of them are healthier and more active and live longer than ever before. We should examine how we may best utilize this unique resource and, where possible incorporate the services of *adoptive grandparents* (my italics) in child-care ...

The National Council for the Unmarried Mother and Her Child also suggested that many families would benefit from being made the concern of a 'granny-figure'. There is nothing tongue-in-cheek about their suggestions that:

A volunteer could fill this role; or older women could be paid for working with families in this way . . .

Can people make themselves into 'granny-figures' by volunteering? And if anyone is to be paid for fulfilling the role, however that role is defined, would it not seem logical to offer the money first to those who merit the title by blood and long, caring relationship? Changes in housing policies require lengthy planning, but if there is finance available for paid 'granny-figures', grants towards telephone calls, public transport and postage costs could do much to keep real families in touch. Perhaps these agencies are right in thinking that all *parents* want of older women is friendship, advice-from-experience, willingness to babysit . . . But what *children* want of grandparents is something quite different. To a young child, a grandmother is unique *because* she is mum's or dad's mother; because she coped with one of them at the age that the child has now reached; because she loved and cared for one of the parents just as they are now loving and caring for the child; because she represents a continuum. An older woman, or an older man, can be an enriching person for a young child to have around. But no volunteer or paid worker can replace the real thing.

Unfortunately the notion that the 'real thing' can be satisfactorily replaced by a state employee or state-sponsored volunteer is not confined to clever ideas about substitute-grannies. Social agencies, brought into discussion by successive governments and by bodies like the CBI and the TUC, recommend unprecedented levels of parent-substitution too. The emphasis in almost every proposal of 'help for families' is on the provision of state-controlled and professionally trained caretakers, of one kind or another, to replace parents. Why? Because those parents are out at work – which, as we have seen, is untrue in the great majority of families – or because they are inadequate, whatever that may mean.

Working Mothers

The official reports state the statistics on the numbers of mothers with children under five who go out to work. But our leaders interpret them and add value-judgements and in doing so they distort the meaning we attach to the facts without ever risking being caught distorting the facts themselves.

During 1978 the Labour Prime Minister made a speech in which he is reported to have said that:

> While the increase in the number of women who work part-time while their children are young is to be applauded, much more help must be given to women who want to work *full-time while their children are under three* (my italics)

Recent reports by the Trades Union Congress and by the Equal Opportunities Commission play the same clever game. They mention an 'increase' in the numbers without stating the tiny percentage from which any increase begins. They talk of the women who 'want' to work full-time, relying on the fact that while there may be many who do not want to do so, there are bound to be enough who do to make their statements 'true'. And then they speak of 'helping' a group whom they have subtly made to sound both enormous and admirable.

Breast-beating, the state agrees with other opinion leaders that its present provision for working mothers is woefully inadequate. That is clever too. If you can persuade public opinion that you *have* a service but that it is not good enough, you will easily be able to persuade people that you have a duty to improve it. If you can be seen to be trying to improve something which you have established as important, you can probably get away with all kinds of measures to which people would object if they had been introduced *de novo*. That is exactly what looks like happening here.

I would argue that the state's service is not merely inadequate but non-existent and that we should therefore give full and wary attention to proposed measures to improve it. Once again the same set of statistics can be used to support either point of view.

Local authority social service departments provide full-time day nursery places for 30,500 children. Of course this is an 'inadequate service' if you compare that figure with even the 172,000 children whose mothers are out for more than thirty hours per week. But it can be argued that these two figures bear no relation to each other because they do not represent the same children. Day nursery places are increasingly reserved for the children of families in crisis, for those who, like the unsupported mother or lone father, live lives of perpetual crisis and for children who are 'at risk' from neglect, squalor or cruelty. Places in day nurseries for the children of mothers who simply want and/or need to take jobs outside their homes are virtually non-existent in most parts of the country. It is difficult to see how these official reports can legitimately present day nurseries as part of even the most inadequate service to working mothers when they themselves recognize this on other pages. It is recommended, for example, that the training of the nursery nurses who staff day nurseries should be changed, to allow for the fact that they now need a 'casework relationship' with virtually all the mothers of their charges.

Most working mothers rely on child-minders. A system of official registration, started in a laudable attempt to reduce abuses, enables local authorities to claim places with child-minders as part of their services to working mothers. In 1976 there were 63,000 full and 20,000 part-time registered places. Estimates of unregistered places are mere guesses derived from the size of the gap between the known number of women at work and the registered ones, with a varying allowance built in for caring fathers and relatives on the one hand and mothers with unofficial jobs on the other. The truth is that child-minding is not a state service, at least not yet.

At present there are no other nationwide state services designed or run for the benefit of mothers who go out to work while their children are below school age but there are a number of services, both state and voluntary, which are designed and run for the benefit of pre-school *children*. It is within these child-orientated services that the authorities see the potential for 'improving' their services to working mothers. Each and every service is threatened with being transformed from something intended to benefit children to something intended to enable those children's parents to go out to work. If mothers want to work outside their homes while their children are very small and if the state or industry wants to provide for them, then let them do so. Let the TUC tell its membership what those proposed 'nursery centres' would actually cost them; let them set them up and see if mothers want to use them. But let all concerned remember just how small the group of mothers who work during this period of their lives is, and ask themselves whether it is equitable to ruin what already exists for children of the millions of mothers who are mothering, for the sake of the thousands who would rather not.

Education is supposed to be for the benefit of those who are being educated. *Ergo*, schools are for children and the organization of our schooling system is at least supposed to be for them. Under the heading of 'help for families' whose children are older than those I am dealing with, the state proposes radical changes designed to bring the length of the school day and term into line with adult working-hours. Call them 'after-school-clubs', 'holiday play-schemes' or what you will. They still amount to keeping children in school, if not at lessons, for almost twice as long in each year of their childhood and not for the sake of their education but for their worker-parents convenience.

But it is not only the education of the children who are already in schools which the state hopes to tamper with. Education is a socio-political 'goody' and you cannot have too much of a good thing. So to 'free' women from full-time child-care earlier and earlier in their children's lives, why not get them into 'education' earlier and earlier?

Starting at the top, legal compulsion still puts them into full-time school when they are five; a year or two younger, one might add, than the children of most industrialized countries. But reorganized admission dates and state encouragement for more reception classes in state infant schools mean that many children must already start when they are four or get out of step with their peers. Some reception classes are run by brilliant teachers with adequate ancillary help and provide superb groups for early social and intellectual learning. But others are not and do not and anyway there is time for schooling, years and years of it.

All three main political parties have also put their support for nursery classes on record. These are nursery schools run on the premises, and under the overall authority, of infant schools. An extraordinarily large number of such schools, unable to find space for an extra classroom to reduce the pupil to teacher ratio higher up, have somehow squeezed a 'temporary' building into the playground to accommodate such a class. Sometimes they function as a 'reception class' and accordingly accommodate four-year-olds, usually with a half-day. But in some schools, formal reception is already at four years so the nursery class takes three-year-olds. Even if the hours are kept short, the adult to child ratio is high and separated playspace is provided, children in these classes are being exposed to an environment whose size, complexity and noise must impinge. When you are three you do not really want to be continually aware of how small you are compared to everybody else. You need to feel big.

State-run nursery schools are a popular vote-catcher too. Despite earlier policies of expansion, government-spending cuts have prevented many from being opened but 'The advantages of nursery education for children from three to five are widely recognized and accepted by the Government' (CPRS) and 'Nursery schooling must be made available to all; indeed the government would like to see facilities extended to all two-year-olds . . .' (the Prime Minister, 1978).

No doubt the government, advised both by social and educational agencies, does truly believe in the *educational* value to children of such classes and schools. But it is clear that their very existence, actual or potential, is also seen as a means of providing care for the benefit of their absent parents. The following extracts from the CPRS report make the state's position clear:

Nursery education absorbs a substantial proportion of expenditure on the under-fives. But the form in which it is provided – short sessions and long holidays – means that it is of little use to many of the mothers and children who need it most. More extended hours and longer sessions in nursery schools would mean that more ... could benefit ...

A flexible and more coordinated service should help the nursery education sector reorientate itself towards the needs of working parents ...

The main recommendation of the study is that the two major services for young children: day nurseries and nursery education, should be reorganized so that both institutions meet the needs of the children concerned for education *and* care rather than maintaining the existing divisions.

Many people, both parents and nursery teachers, would argue that the last quoted 'main recommendation' is impossible because an institution which meets children's 'needs' for education *and* for day-care is a contradiction in terms. A good nursery group, admitting only children who are ready, socially, emotionally and intellectually, both to get something from group-life and to give something to it, can be excellent experience for a child for three hours per day, five days per week, thirty-six weeks in the year. But extending its hours and its terms alters and may well ruin it. The demands made on both children and teachers will be increased beyond their tolerance. Teachers will rightly resent being employed as babysitters and may well find cause for complaint if they are asked to fulfil their educative role in a baby-minding setting, even if nursery nurses are employed to staff it. Above all, nursery education groups which are turned into a service for working mothers will lose their prime orientation towards meeting children's needs.

Voluntary organizations must be even more rightfully infuriated by the state take-over bid which, in many instances, involves keeping and using their efforts, but in ways and towards ends which they specifically disapprove. Perhaps the most glaring example in this report concerns playgroups run by

27

the Pre-School Playgroups Association. There are more children under five in these playgroups than in any other form of pre-school provision. The organization exists:

> To help parents to understand and provide for the needs of their young children. It aims to promote community situations in which parents can with growing enjoyment and confidence make the best uses of their own knowledge and resources in the development of their children and themselves.

It is, as one member put it, 'A voluntary organization but each playgroup is a self-help group . . .'

During 1976, 1977 and 1978, the PPAs playgroups suffered from the lowering of the age of school entry and the opening of a few state nursery schools and classes. The first drained off their four-year-olds. The second provided some parents, ignorant of the radical difference between a playgroup and a nursery school, with places for their children *which were free.* The results were some unbalanced books and empty places alongside the usual queue of parents desperate to get toddlers admitted. The PPAs constitution says that its playgroups are 'primarily for children of three or over'. But the temptation of those empty places, the threat of closure from those unbalanced books, the emotional pressure from those queueing parents and the let-out of that word 'primarily' proved too much for some playgroup organizers. Two-year-olds were admitted and controversy raged as controversy only can in an organization as democratically decentralized as the PPA. Eventually it was decided that children under three should not, for their own and other children's sakes, join PPA groups.

But just as it sees nursery schools in existence and at once plans to remake them into a part of day-care, so the state sees playgroups flourishing and sees how to 'integrate' them too. The first remark concerning playgroups in the CPRS report runs totally counter to the aims of the PPA:

> One of the more important benefits of the spread of playgroups . . . is the opportunity they give to hard-pressed parents to have a break from the demands of small children . . .

The plans for playgroups, outlined in the policy section of the report, actually reverse the P P As own painstakingly decided policy:

As nursery education expands, the role of playgroups could be developed to concentrate especially on the younger ages, including those under three . . .

The recent Equal Opportunities Commission report was overtly scathing about playgroups. Totally ignoring their stated role in providing something for *children and parents* – and totally ignoring the fact that, given the numbers on the rolls, what they provide must be something parents want – they categorized them as useless because they do not provide for *working* mothers. Last week, the Association of Head Teachers' report similarly ignored the value of parent participation in playgroups by sniffily asserting that they were 'no alternative to proper nursery schools run by qualified teachers . . .'

Mother-and-toddler clubs are not regarded as part of the 'education' scene because there is not yet any such profession as mother-and-toddler-club-person. But even these informal, community-based groups, which wax and wane with the enthusiasm of a wide range of individuals and voluntary organizations, are grist to the mill of the CPRS report. While acknowledging them as places where mothers can find company for themselves as well as their children, and while unable to suggest adaptations which would make them useful to working mothers, it still suggests to such groups the one role which most of them would reject: '. . . mothers can soon pop out for a break, leaving their children safely . . .'

It does seem that the official version of 'help for families' is 'facilities to enable mothers to go out to work'. Existing organizations whose stated purpose is to benefit children educationally are to be twisted around so that they can replace, rather than add to, parental care. Even organizations established by parents to help themselves to parent better and more happily are to be deformed into the mould of an escape route.

29

Underprivileged Families

Britain has many families which are, perhaps euphemistically, described as 'underprivileged'. Most of them are poor – with all that that implies in a materialistic society committed to a growth economy. Others are variously: ill – physically and/or mentally; culturally displaced; incompetent; unfortunate ... Sir Keith Joseph coined a neat phrase, the 'cycle of deprivation' to describe the observed but little-understood probability that an 'underprivileged family' will produce 'underprivileged children' who will, in their turn, produce more. Breaking this cycle has become an unimpeachable aspiration for concerned professionals and a natural for public speakers. The many professional bodies which find themselves concerned with families whose problems seem insurmountable, not only to those who must suffer them but also to those who try to relieve them, are honest about their ignorance of causation and their helplessness to cure. Nevertheless, such families give rise to endless emergencies which have to be coped with somehow, by someone. And the bitter realization that each piece of professional work merely plugs one small hole in a sieve makes 'preventative measures' seem extremely attractive.

I suspect that the search for the cause and cure for 'multiple deprivation' may be similar to the search for the cause and cure of cancer, both being multiply-caused multiple-ills. But the state is dedicated to preventative measures and convinced that they *can* prevent. Babies and young children, as obviously innocent victims now and as the obvious hope or expense for the future, are the favourite recipients of special attention:

Preventative work undertaken with under-fives and their families can reduce the waste of expensive resources at a later stage, when the need to cope with the consequences of family stress and breakdown becomes more apparent and urgent, as the children are involved in delinquency, crime, truancy or exhibit emotional problems ...

So says the CPRS and it rests heavily on the court report 'Fit for the Future' (1977)

Preventative work with young children is an intensely difficult area for professional workers because emotions, their own, the child's, the family's and those evoked by media-reporting, tend to blur the issues and smear the results. A toddler, hospitalized for that other euphemism 'non-accidental injury', wrings everyone's heart. If he cries for his parents and they cry for him, the pressure to let him return home is strongly felt by everybody. But the tears may have little to do with the issue of prevention, either in the short-term sense of preventing further physical injury to the child, or in the long-term sense of preventing further social problems emanating from the family. If he is sent home he may, or may not, be hurt again. If he is kept 'in care' he will be physically safe but nobody can know that he would not have been so back with his parents. Against the possibility that he has been saved from further injury or from death has to be weighed the certainty of a heavy financial cost to the state and an unknown emotional cost to the child himself and to his family. For the professionals, it is a no-win situation and one in which the media are usually quick to give an adverse opinion whatever decision is made.

In such highly-charged situations of uncertain outcome, the state's belief that its intervention can truly alter the course of children's lives often seems to be compounded equally of faith and economy. Multiply-deprived families are poor, whatever else they may or may not be. Left to struggle on through their difficulties with the long-term help of professional case-workers, they will cost benefits and professional time in the present and continuing benefits plus costly trouble with the growing children later. If the children are taken out of their parents' care, whether full-time for placement in a children's or foster-home, or daily, into one of those priority day nursery places, both parents can go to work. In theory they thus relieve their own poverty and save the state from paying whatever benefits they had been receiving. In theory, too, the children will be saved from their adverse family circumstances and the 'cycle of deprivation' will be broken. In practice things seldom work out quite like that. Jobs are hard, now, for many people to find so the benefit payments to the multiply-deprived family may well have to continue. As to the prevention of later difficulties in the children: there is no evidence that I know of to suggest that state intervention works.

A desire for families to earn money to live on rather than being given it by the state often leads to the expenditure of disproportionate amounts of state money on child-care. I suspect a combination of puritanism, compartmentalized accounting and authoritarian belief that poor children are better off in nice, clean institutions. For example the CPRS report clearly states that in November 1976 the capital cost per child of a place in a day nursery was £3,800 with annual running costs per child of £1,130. Yet one of the six groups of families who should receive priority in getting these places for their children is: 'Single parents who are *not seeking employment*' (my italics). The clear implication is that such a day nursery place will enable the parent to look for a job and will, indeed, enable those responsible for his or her benefit Giro to reduce it if no employment is sought. Yet how much money could such a lone parent be realistically expected to feed back into the economy? Certainly nothing comparable with the cost of having the child cared for by the state. Surely there can be no pretence here of 'helping families'? That lone parent is not being helped in the almost-impossible task of being a family all alone. Instead the state is manoeuvring the financial situation so as to enforce separation between parent and child.

Who is Left?

So the children of Britain's immediate future are to go into educational institutions even earlier than they do now and stay there for longer so that both their parents can work. Those who are too young, even by British standards, for full-time schooling are to benefit from 'pre-school education' which, in some miraculous way, is to be combined with adequate day-care so that both their parents can work. Eventually this pre-school system is to be made available to all two-year-olds but, in the meantime, existing provisions for parents *and* children are to be reformed to provide some work possibilities for both parents and the needs of priority groups of under-fives for full-time day-care are to be met as a matter of urgency.

So who is left out? Only our babies. Judging by the enthusiasm with which the Departments of Health, Education and Social Security have been talking of 'a complete and integrated service for all children under five' it will not be long before they too are involved in this horrendous dream. The details of such a service are not yet fully worked out. Central government is all too aware that, even with the aid of earmarked block-grants, local authorities cannot, and will not, do everything immediately. But the circular letter 'Coordination of services for children under five' (DHSS 1978) clearly implies that the state *should* make provision for every aspect of children's welfare from birth until their passing into the expert hands of the compulsory school system. The government recognizes that nobody can afford to jettison the mish-mash of services, state and voluntary, presently available on a varying scale to the parents of under-threes. But each and every one of them is to be gathered into a centralized scheme of surveillance and advice.

Day nurseries are seen as the core-organizations which: 'can serve as a focus for all day-care services in their areas'. The government recommends that sponsored day-minding and day-fostering schemes should be brought under their wings and that links should be developed between day nurseries, nursery schools and classes, playgroups, mother-and-toddler groups and all voluntary associations working in any way with the under-fives 'to ensure that the fullest use is made of the experience of staff working in the nursery . . .'

Health surveillance, by health visitors, is to be increased and health visitors 'need to coordinate the care given to a child at home and in day-care . . .'

Playgroups, which must already register with social services departments, are to receive 'support and guidance' from special staff members within those departments. Their names and addresses are to be notified to the area nurse (child health) at the department. Playgroups are differentiated in terms of whether or not those who are involved in running them have been trained as teachers or social workers. All, but especially those whose organizers have no such training – being simply mothers – should be in contact with schools and the local education authority. Playgroups are statedly seen as interim provision standing in for the state nursery classes which would be opened if there was the money to do so. Accordingly, as many as possible should now be placed in primary schools (whose falling role often leaves spare classrooms) so as to be safely under the wing of 'education'.

Child-minders, rightly seen as the best day-carers for very young children, are to receive compulsory in-service training. They are also to receive financial support 'to underline the advantages of registration and so assist authorities in introducing minimum requirements . . .' They are to have close liaison with the health authorities and close links with child health clinics and with nursery schools and classes. Day-fostering, as a fully professional service, is to be encouraged, especially where numbers of children do not justify the building of a day nursery. Even closer liaison is presented as an ideal:

One authority is planning a day nursery with a group of child-minders attached, who will be supervised by the nursery. The nursery will provide a back-up service for holidays and periods of illness and emphasis is also put on provision for families, particularly where mothers need support in the care of their children.

Mother-and-baby clubs are seen as 'complementing playgroup and nursery school provision'. Clubs have been set up in child health clinics and infant schools by a number of local authorities and voluntary agencies 'as well as by the mothers themselves'. Such groups should also be provided with supervision and advice by the local authority.

There is no doubt that 'combined centres' of various types are the government's ideal. The more everything and everybody to do with young children can be gathered together for proper expert guidance, surveillance and control, the better. While paying reiterated lip-service to the importance of working with, rather than against, parents, all these documents make it clear that the state feels that as well as helping those parents who cannot cope, and say so, it has a duty to act for other parents too, because in some way organization and expertise is preferable to individualistic amateurism in dealing with small children.

Parents do not always agree. The various social agencies who contribute most to governmental discussion and policy-making in this area are accustomed to trying to persuade people to accept what the state thinks best for them rather than what they actually want. In the DHSS report 'Preparation for Parenthood' the consulted agencies agreed that:

... the majority of parents would not participate in a parent education movement or attend formal further or adult education classes even if, as was suggested, they were given a financial incentive to attend.

A variety of measures designed to get parents within hearing distance of the advice being offered to them, were suggested. They ranged from 'tea and buns' through 'free hair-do's' to actual money. It was left to the Association of Community Workers to voice the widespread idea of actual subterfuge:

... a major obstacle has been a feeling of 'us/them' ... It is important that a wide range of community groups be recognized as legitimate and desirable, including such bodies as Tenants' Associations [sic!] ... *Statutory support cannot be totally disguised* (my italics) but it can be brought as close as possible to local people by the appointment of ... neighbourhood-based workers with minimal constraints placed upon their activities by the employing authority ...

This paragraph sums up much of the state's present approach to parents and their young children and epitomizes the attitudes which lead me to describe 'help for families' as a con. The phrase 'us and them' is used in common parlance to describe a feeling that we are in some way distanced from an authoritative 'them' which is not tuned in to our feelings or needs. But here it is reversed. 'Us' is the authority, which genuinely believes that it knows and wants what is best for parents and their children. 'Them' is the parents, who will not listen and behave as the authority wishes even though it tries so hard to make them believe that it does not consider itself in any way 'superior' to them!

It has not been the experience of self-help groups (and I include the PPA as the longest established, most widespread and obviously successful of them all) that the majority of parents refuse to participate in anything which is *of their own making*. When the state has to bribe and cover its tracks to persuade adults to do something for their own good, it is just possible that their view of their good differs from the state's and that it might be the one who needs to think again. 'Everyone's out of step but our Johnny . . .'

I believe that while a new awareness of the needs of young children and their parents is long overdue, this interpretation of their problems and the consequent approach to their solution is totally wrong-headed.

Babies and young children need parents, or other special individual people to whom they can relate as parents. They need at least one of these more or less full-time during the whole of their first three years. They need the same ones always available, before, between and after brief forays into group situations, after that. Only in exceptional circumstances can it be right for any state authority – or self-styled expert – to take over responsibility for even part of a very young child's care.

But I do not believe that this primary need of young human beings is the intolerable burden on mothers that people would have us believe, because I do not believe that the need is all one way around. Mothers also need their babies and small children and few are comfortable with minimal mothering although some are stuck with it and more are threatened. Leaving a very young child who clearly wants you and whose need you can feel, is a special kind of hell. What feels right and comfortable to most mothers is to be usually available to a child until he himself begins to want to leave his mother on the adventurings that are an increasing part of being three and four and five . . .

These views are unfashionable. The women's movement spokespeople have seen to that. But women's lib and mothers' lib are not the same. We urgently need to sort out the one from the other.

3. Women's Lib and Mothers' Lib

All mothers are women but not all women are mothers. The people who are both are trapped, politically, socially and economically. The new people they produce are suffering and, through them and the next generation they will produce when they grow up, the whole of society will suffer unless we can free them.

For a long time now women have been asserting themselves for their self-evident rights as full people; equals in opportunities, pay and power, in public and in private, with men. But in their determination to assert their potential as sex-irrelevant persons – whether by driving a bus, wearing a dog collar, carrying a mortgage or simply living without a male – they have ignored, or even tried to deny, the one role which is, and must remain, uniquely female: mothering.

Instead of making decent circumstances for creative mothering a part of their package of demanded rights, many advocates of the women's movement have put motherhood on one side as a tiresome and irrelevant barrier to being exactly like men. When such spokespeople are faced with the biological necessity for women to continue to become mothers, they tend to acknowledge the biology without acknowledging the emotional commitment which is part and parcel of it. 'Having a baby should not make any difference to a woman's self-fulfilment in every other sphere . . .' they say. Or even 'Having a baby should not make any difference to a woman's life . . .' And there, at the first big women's liberation movement march in London, were the banners demanding 'day nurseries for all'. Faced with the suggestion that perhaps women who do not want children to affect their self-fulfilment or alter their lives should avoid having any children in the first place, such spokespeople tend to resort to the female chauvinism of: 'any woman has a right to have a baby if she wants to because the ability to do so is part of her potential as a female person . . .' To me such statements are a sad doublethink and unworthy of a movement which has done so much to make people think about the social roles we all tend to take for granted.

All human beings have the potential for innumerable kinds of activity. Yet in every other area of life we all accept that, far from having a 'right' to fulfil every one which may occur to us, we have an absolute duty to curb many. We all carry the potential for murderous violence. Yet who will speak out for my 'rights' when I act that one out? Even on the basis of strict sex-equality alone, the assertion of a woman's right to have babies makes no sense. Most men have the potential to father as many children as they can find females to impregnate. Both sexes have worked long and hard to ensure that they do not do so.

We are social beings. We have individual rights but they cannot rightfully be exercised at the expense of other individuals' rights. If women insist on being treated just as men are treated while still insisting on having babies as and when they please, they put themselves in an untenable position and they deny the rights of the new people they produce. That the position is untenable – or at least often intolerable – is shown by the confusion, exhaustion and constant guilt of women who are trying to hold down a 'real' job while coping with offspring. Getting pregnant, even having the baby, is comparatively easy or at least quickly over. But once it is done, the baby is there and goes on being there; existing; relentlessly determined to become the person he or she has every right to be. That the rights of such children are often denied is shown by the monstrous regularity with which they get themselves killed, maimed, rejected, emotionally or intellectually stunted.

I am being dramatic and I mean to be because so far the colourful and emotive writing has all been on the side of those 'liberationists' who want to see *all* women, mothers or not, out in the commercial jungle proving something.

A recent edition of a widely-read women's liberation magazine described the full-time care of a baby or very young child as:

Like spending all day, every day, in the exclusive company of an incontinent mental defective.

It was not like that for me and I do not believe that it is like that for most women. What I do believe is that the rearing of babies and young children is, and if it is to be satisfactory for all concerned, should be, a highly involving and creative business. It cannot be well and happily done as an afterthought to a life which is already both practically and emotionally full. Trying to do it in that way is like trying to produce a gourmet meal out of cans. I also believe that a great many women – and some of their partners too – would find it a tremendous relief if this were acknowledged publicly. While no doubt many do so acknowledge it to themselves, they cannot easily come right out and say so because the image of the wholehearted mother has become so rectangularly square. It will not be long before jokes about 'mums' replace those old ones about 'mothers-in-law'.

But of course magazines and writers like that one do not represent the whole of our society. Surely a more balanced view of the nature and needs of young children is being presented somewhere? Yes indeed, but not where it is most noticeable to most people. The headline stories of even the more intellectual elements of the mass media suggest that even among 'responsible' social leaders and commentators the mutual need of children for their mothers and mothers for their children has been forgotten. A random selection made during a single month in 1978 produced the following stories:

Opposition MPs shout for a reduction in the age of criminal responsibility because two boys of four and six violently assaulted an old woman and frightened her into a fatal heart attack. They would like to be able to protect society from these dangerous infants by having powers to put them in 'secure accommodation'. But what is forgotten in this passionate reaction after an appalling event, is that every infant is potentially dangerous, to himself and to other people, if he or she is left without continuous external control by a responsible adult before internal controls have fully developed. So every infant needs to be in 'secure accommodation'. It is called home.

They would like another change in the law, those righteous men. A change which would enable them to punish the parents. But for what? For being out at the jobs the government, the economic situation and public opinion are all pressing them to take? Controlling a baby and young child, keeping him safe and keeping his behaviour acceptable to other people, is an important part of being a parent and it is a creative part too. By showing the child, again and again, what behaviour is safe and acceptable, by preventing the behaviours that are not, parents build up a structure in the child's mind which will, eventually, control his behaviour when there is nobody there to tell him what he should or should not do. He takes the instructions of these outside people into himself. Control from others turns, gradually, into self-control. Disapproval from others turns into guilt. Punishment turns into the pricks and pangs of what we call conscience. But it all takes a long time and a lot of steady, continuous work. Children are neither good nor bad by 'nature' or 'instinct'. They can only become what we regard as 'socialized' by being in constant contact with adult representatives of their society until such time as that society's values have become part of them. Absent parents cannot, by definition, be in constant contact and those particular children had not internalized our prohibitions against violence sufficiently to maintain them when they were on their own. If they were late in doing so, if most six-year-olds would find it impossible to take a brick to an old woman's head, it is probably because that continuous contact had been lacking all through the peak socialization period since babyhood.

A three-year-old girl, on her way home from the shops, is raped and murdered. The media have a field day of horror but nobody except the shopkeeper, who worried about her enough to see her across the road, asks the really important question: How did a child of this age come to be out in the streets alone?

A baby, one of many in this as in every month, is battered, hospitalized, returned home and killed. Another field day, but this time let's blame the social workers. Again, for what? We may, or may not, depending on your point of view, be short of trained social workers. But however many we have, state employees are never going to be able to mount twenty-four-hour duty in every home where a child is thought to be 'at risk'; much less protect children in the thousands of homes where, unbeknownst to the state, parents are finding life impossible. In this expert-ridden society it is easy to see the answer to any problem as lying in an increase of available professionals. But short of substituting a trained mother-substitute for every natural mother whom we have invited to sidestep mothering, no amount of social work is going to protect our young from the results of our social ineptitude.

The social problems families are facing cannot be prevented or cured by increasing dollops of professional social work or variegated counselling. These things, good in themselves when rightly used, do not produce a socially-sane society. Indeed it can be argued that their increase parallels a diminishing of society's sanity. This is a lesson which we could have learned from the history of the National Health Service. Beveridge truly believed that a comprehensive, free-at-time-of-consultation, health service for all would gradually work itself out of business. He believed that by coping with all the backlog of ill-health in society a state of positive good health could be achieved. It has not happened. The medical professions have elucidated more ills and more treatments and cures; more and more people have subjected themselves to all three. At the present rate of expansion, that health service could be employing half the labouring population to look after the other half by the end of the century. We are in danger of falling into exactly the same trap with the other helping professions.

Being a human being means living in a family, group, community and society. It is a complicated business and it always has been. I cannot pretend to know what being a nomadic prehistoric person was like, but complexity is a safe bet. But managing that complicated business is what being human is all about. Very gradually, often so insidiously that nobody can decide exactly where and when to call 'stop!', the ability to manage, even the right to try to manage, is slipping away from us.

If this were being brought about by obvious forces of accepted evil – perhaps by authoritarian governments whose legislation was enforced by thugs – it would be easy to recognize the enemy and to see how to go about combating it. But in the western world the trend towards reliance on and control by 'them' is far more subtle than that. Increasing knowledge and technical and technological know-how have brought tremendous benefits. Education and the mass media have ensured that we know of these benefits. Knowing of them we naturally want them for ourselves and our children. So our demand increases and so does the supply of modern goodies. Nobody means any harm. Nobody is trying to force us at gunpoint. We are the ones whose expectations include continuous rises in our 'standards of living'. We are the ones who increasingly seek freedom from one set of 'problems' and thus create another. Freedom from child-care produces the problems of the working mother. In just the same way freedom from a long working week is producing something called 'the problem of leisure' . . .

The real problem is that these advances have complicated the lives of all of us to a point where we cannot provide the good things we see to be available for ourselves. In almost every area of life, the best that there is can only be had with the help of expert specialists.

Take a farmer who aims to make the best living he can from his crops and his livestock. In the past, even the quite recent past, he did this by the application of knowledge and skill passed on to him by other farmers. He used care and hard work. He used trial and error. He did his best and sometimes he succeeded beyond his expectations, sometimes he failed for reasons he could see and avoid next time, sometimes he failed for reasons beyond his control or beyond his comprehension. But now that farmer knows that his land and his stock can produce more and more for his family through the application of modern techniques. The techniques may, or may not, be within his understanding, but they are certainly beyond his practising abilities. Soil analysis will tell him exactly which chemical to apply to the land for maximum yields of specific crops. But he can neither analyse the soil nor make the chemical fertilizers for himself. Immunization and specialized balancing of food-concentrate intake to milk or egg output or bodyweight will keep his stock healthy and ensure that they produce maximum amounts of human food for minimum amounts of money. But the farmer cannot produce the veterinary drugs nor administer them; he cannot even grow many of the foodstuffs. Cows do not eat grass and hay these days, they eat fish. So the farmer needs a lot of expert help and to make it all easy for him the same agricultural expert will make the tests and sell him the fertilizers, the drugs and the manufactured foods. His yields shoot up to a point where transportation and marketing become specialized too, so he will be tied into a collection and distribution system in the name of the god Efficiency.

For the individual farmer and for the country's economy as a whole, all this is clearly beneficial. Of course he must fight to keep his increased profits ahead of his increased expenditure; of course he may sometimes wonder why, with dairy cows on the place, his family cannot have fresh cream without buying it from a shop, but overall he is doing something which is clearly sensible. He is making more money for less uncertainty and less gruelling work. And he is doing his bit in keeping viable an economy which depends on importing Peruvian fish to feed to animals in order to export butter to Europe. It is because the personal good sense is so obvious that the personal loss of independence and self-confidence is so difficult to pin down so that it can be weighed in any kind of balance. I stood recently with one farmer and watched the Bird's Eye machines cropping the pea-fields to which his land is now devoted. 'It's not like it was,' he said tentatively. Quick as a flash a neighbour came back with a 'Got the "good ol' days blues" have you, Bill? Come on, nobody's got time to shuck those buggers these days . . .'

Perhaps a loss of independent self-confidence in the jobs that we do is tolerable. Certainly farmers maintained it for far longer than most people, who lost it with the establishment of the factory production line. Perhaps it is possible for us to lead satisfactory lives with a total split between what we do to make money and what we choose to do during the leisure hours that money-making leaves us. But a similar pattern can be seen, for similar reasons, in our personal and inter-personal lives. It is here that it hits hardest at the people who are most involved in personal relationships, especially those with an element of dependency.

An elderly relative becomes infirm, perhaps incontinent, certainly incapable of looking after herself. We know that there are trained health visitors and home helps whose job it is to help and we turn automatically to them. Surely it would be irresponsible not to seek the best care that is available? Surely we should be committing the crime of failing to fulfil ourselves if we substituted our own non-expert care, thus tying ourselves down with the responsibility for another human being?

A new baby, *our* baby, cries and does not gain much weight. We want to do the very best for him and there is the clinic with its trained staff and its weighing machines and its tables of 'ideal weight gain'. Surely it is only right to consult them? Surely they will tell us exactly how to mix a scientific food-formula which, given in the right quantities, will 'make' that baby grow at the approved rate? Anyway we want to know why he keeps crying and what we should do about it. Surely the easiest way to find out is to ask the people who 'know about babies'? There are other ways. We could ask the baby what he wants to eat and how much and when. We could ask him, by trial and error, why he cries and what will help him not to. But it would take time. It would take self-involvement. We might get interested and bore other people by talking about him. We might even, heaven forfend, 'turn into cows'. No, modern motherhood is not supposed to swallow women up and have them thinking about their babies all the time. There are people who are trained to do that.

Do not misunderstand me. Most of the 'experts' who enter

every corner of our lives really do have a great deal to offer to those who need them. Expert advances really are advances, they work. I am not deriding those who use them; that farmer wants more yield and, with expert help, he can have it. I am not deriding those who provide them either. That baby might not be getting enough to eat for his personal needs-of-the-moment and if he is hungry and his parents do not know it, somebody had better suggest it to them fast. I have no romantic image of life in medieval, Victorian or pre-war Britain; no desire to put the clock back. But I am worried about what the very existence and skills of all those professionals do to ordinary people, never forgetting that outside their own little areas of competence, the experts are ordinary people too.

Once there are experts in almost every field and once everyone knows that there are, two vitally important things seem to happen:

Whatever it is that the experts have to offer is wanted by everyone whether they actually 'need' it or not. And each person can make out an unimpeachable case for having it.

The very existence of a body of expertise makes people outside the speciality feel inadequate and, far more important, makes them take their own inadequacy for granted.

So the more expert-ridden a society becomes, the faster some people turn for 'help' and the guiltier others feel for not doing so. 'Helping oneself' becomes a matter of getting around to consulting an expert and much of the energy which might have gone into personal problem-solving goes instead into righteous wrath when those expert resources prove to be thinly-spread through the community. Hence: 'There's nothing I can do for her, she wouldn't even let the Welfare in . . .' and 'He's only himself to blame, he won't go to the doctor . . .' Hence, too, 'Look at that paper peeling off the wall. Six months we've been waiting for the Council to put that right . . .' and 'Come home? Yes, they said she could come home, but who's going to see to her when that nurse doesn't turn up?'

The more people feel that the answers to their human and personal problems rightly lie with professionals, the less they listen to and trust themselves and the less they listen to and trust each other. Some of the letters I receive from parents demonstrate this clearly. Rare gems will say something like: 'We have talked and talked about this but we still aren't sure we are doing the best thing . . .'

A lengthy description of what they are doing and of the evidence for and against it will follow. They have met a problem; recognized it as such; talked about it with other concerned people and then, only then, decided to add an 'expert' opinion into the decision-making balance. But most of the letters start straight in with a blunt request for authoritative instruction: 'Shall I smack her when she . . .?' or for guidance as to what is, or is not, a problem: 'Is my baby getting spoiled?' The tragedy is that the writers truly believe that I shall know better than they do. My supposed 'expertise' outweighs their knowledge of, and love for, a child whom I have never even met.

People do not only come into contact with the 'experts', and with the people who think they know how people should think of themselves, when they seek private consultations. In our society a tremendous volume of information is poured straight into people's homes through television, radio, newspapers, books . . .

While everybody can try to look, listen and read selectively, no one of us can absorb all the information that is pressed upon us nor hope to judge rightly whom to take notice of and whom to ignore. So we all tend to listen most to those who shout loudest. And, because the media have a certain glamour of their own, we all start out with a sneaking feeling that anyone who gets a lot of television exposure or space in a national newspaper must have something sensible to say. Many of them do. But what they say is inevitably selected by programmers and editors and part of the selection procedure must have to do with fashion and trend. So the media tend both to latch on to subjects, attitudes and people which are fashionable, and to make them fashionable by exposing them to millions. An idea that started as just that, an idea, gets itself made into a creed. The person who presented the idea gets made into an 'expert'. And we all believe it.

Although the media are vast in their reach and influence they are tiny in their personnel. There are incalculably large numbers of people whose ideas, whose voices, are never heard at all. And there are even larger numbers who never give voice because they have no reason to believe that anybody wants to listen to them. A few, a very few, parents in the first group write to me or telephone to radio phone-ins. Even some of the second group will talk, around the shops and the playgroups, the day nurseries, school gates and playgrounds, if they discover that somebody is actually listening to them.

Their points of view are often totally different from the media-canvassed and therefore socially-accepted views. Sadly, awareness of the difference does not make most people angry or even eager to be heard. It makes them guilty. If they cannot do, or feel, or be, what the media suggest, then it must be they, not the media, who are out of step. I wish that an equal balance of currently fashionable and trendy views and these private ones could be presented. I am not saying that anyone or any view is 'right' or 'wrong' or even desirable or undesirable. I am simply saying that the public picture is lop-sided. If it could be centred, as real life centres everything, many private people would feel freer to be, and happier about being, themselves.

A widely-read and rightly popular female journalist wrote about having a baby alone, with no male help after, we must presume, impregnation. Her message was that she had done it, was rearing the child alone and was marvellously happy about it all. 'You can do it too,' she said and the clear implication was that it was a 'good' thing to do.

For every one of that journalist there are many thousands of women who actually have to manage babies and children alone. The ones who write, or speak, to me do not like it and do not think that it is good for the children. They seem to have an old-fashioned (or could it be going to be a new-fashioned?) feeling that mothers have a better life with partners around and that children do better with two parents, one of whom is pretty constantly available. They do not feel especially proud of the accomplishment of single parenthood. Many of them did not engineer the role and wish that contraceptive failure, divorce or death had not wished it on them. Even the few who did choose it in one way or another rarely see their lives as a strike for independent womanhood. If their minds are on strikes at all it is of another kind.

Hang around for a few early morning hours at the entrance to a state day nursery and you will see these views borne out by the many mothers who would not dream of expressing them to anyone. Only a minute proportion (and I am being careful; it is so small as to be often invisible) of the mothers you see dropping off their babies and small children are gleefully shaking off the bonds of motherhood to hurry to yet another fulfilling professional day. The vast majority are grimly facing yet another stint at a tedious and repetitive job, always conscious of the child they have left and never therefore able to give themselves entirely to the adult world.

A television programme at peak-viewing time extolled father-participation and role-swapping between sexual partners as the obvious answer to giving all family members what they want and ought to have. Outside those studios and screens there are countless families which can only keep their heads above the state poverty line if father holds down a job. High falutin' nonsense about sharing that job with his partner so as to take an equal share in the care of their children would get him the push as soon as the laughter died down. There are too many men in the benefit queue. With unemployment high and rising, why should employers take even a little trouble to enable people to double up? With steady jobs scarce, why should a family risk one for a new venture? With those queues there are also families in which the mother can get a job and the father cannot. The compulsory role-swapping which often follows does not seem to give much pleasure either. As one woman put it: 'Our children have a mother they see in the evening and at week-ends and a male substitute-mother who is around most of the time. What they don't have is either a mother or a father . . .'

A mass-circulation paperback appeared telling women how to combine a fascinating career with exceptionally stimulating care for an (inevitably) brilliant toddler. It is only when you have digested the glowing description of returning home, intellectually refreshed, self-fulfilled, and all the readier to play word-games with the baby, that you pause to wonder who gave him his lunch or who, indeed, gave him his first words. If a job is hugely enjoyable and pays enough to enable a mother to buy herself a substitute-mother to care for her child then she is fortunate and she should not need a book to tell her how to manage. Most women find themselves tired, rather than refreshed, by their jobs; there is nothing intellectually stimulating about typing invoices or putting cherries on cakes. Very few earn enough to pay for individual nannies, or even au pairs, for their children, so if it is work for them it is care outside the home for the kids. Furthermore there is not much time for word-games – or any other kind of fun – if mother and child do not get home from the nursery or the minder until 6 or 7 p.m. and there is still a meal to get amid last night's crumbs . . .

Somehow society has to give people back their confidence in being able to manage being people for themselves amid the actual reality of their own circumstances. The women's movement has formed and re-formed groups, dedicated to the idea of helping women to be themselves and to feel free of the traditional pressures of what anybody else may expect, or want them to be. Its influence has been tremendous, and largely beneficial for women who are trying to find and assert themselves as individual human beings. But that same influence has been unrealistic and even destructive to women who are trying to be mothers, because being a mother is not an individualistic business but a duality. The ideal of self-awareness flourishes but many women find that it does not mesh with the reality of being a real, caring human being. And real, caring human beings are what many women actually *want to be*. One member of a women's group, also a mother, put it like this:

I'm coming to the conclusion that at the moment I can't be very interested in the idea of *me* as a separate entity. In fact I don't really think that there is a 'me' which isn't all mixed up with the children and their father; all the people I care about and have made part of me and given bits of myself to. I tried to put it to the group because surely if I'm to be free to be whatever I want to be, I ought to be free to be that kind of person – someone whose main thing-of-the-moment is mothering. But it was hopeless. They all thought I was doing the self-sacrificing wife-and-mother bit. I wasn't. I was doing a no-man-is-an-island bit . . . .

All mothers are women first and always. But the chunk of time which they choose to spend giving to, and receiving from, children, constitutes a special role and has special needs. I should like to see the women's movement continue to concentrate its powers on the formation of young women with genuine freedom of choice in their lives. But I should also like to see it acknowledge that some will freely choose to spend some of their lives in mothering and that those who do, merit its support and its campaigns to exactly the same degree as those who do not. As long as being a mother to the best of her ability is seen as some kind of betrayal of feminist ideals, the women's movement will fail as a movement for women as people and remain a movement for particular kinds of women only. While it remains so we shall continue to hear the tragic messages of women like this one who bravely put in print:

I feel that I have tried and tried to do something difficult with my life and it has all gone wrong . . . I realized with relief and horror mixed together that I *was* a lot of the things I had spent ten years despising with all my heart. I actually yearned to spend whole days gurgling at a baby instead of arguing with intelligent, articulate contemporaries . . . God help us, I wanted a husband . . .

That article, in a national daily paper, was signed 'a self-confessed feminist who has failed'.

4. Mothers' Rights

The ability to carry and give birth to babies gives women an inbuilt advantage over men whose procreative role begins and ends in a single orgasm. Without those nurtured foetuses there can be no babies and it is women who nurture and can be seen to nurture them. Without those babies there can be no new people and it is women who deliver them and can be seen to do so. Without new people there can be no society for either sex to dominate.

Despite the obviousness of this one-upwomanship it is unusual to hear child-bearing potential described as any kind of advantage because historically it was an extremely dubious privilege. A baby a year; half of them dead before their names went into the family Bible and the mother more likely to die in agonizing obstructed labour than from rampant and uncontrolled disease ... No wonder motherhood was seen as one of women's many burdens, along with 'the curse', men's 'gross appetites' and everything connected with sexuality.

But now things are different. They really have changed. I labour the point both because it is vital to my argument and because I can already hear the articulate cries of rage the statement will provoke. Yes, everyone can contradict this stand. There are the ruined lives of babies nobody wanted and of the women who did not want them. There are the women whose abortions led to sterility. There are women who are drowning in the black pools of continuing postnatal depression. There are families tethered by handicapped children and handicapped children who, tethers severed, are lost in the wards of long-stay institutions. All of these and many more are still part of the tragedy of motherhood. And individually they make me cry and rage as much as anyone. But I still say that things have changed, that motherhood has become a privilege rather than a burden because overall, with modern contraception and the abortion laws of this country, *women do not have to have children if they do not want them.*

To be a woman, even a married woman, is no longer prescriptive of being a mother. To be a liberated woman is to have and to use the option of remaining childless, of separating sex from procreation. So for me, the first and the most important part of any mothers' liberation movement is *the right not to be one.*

There are still a great many unwanted babies born in Britain so clearly the right of choice is not yet being fully exercised. The reasons which are usually put forward are the difficulty of educating women into the use of safe contraceptives and the intransigency of male gynaecologists faced with requests for abortion. But I do not believe that either one constitutes the real barrier. Women who have truly decided, all the way through themselves, not to get pregnant, need not. There is usually more than a touch of ambivalence in the girl who decided to 'risk it' or the married woman who forgets her pill. When contraceptives do fail – and I am not denying that they can, sometimes – women who are self-confidently sure that they want the foetus aborted can and do find doctors who are ready to oblige. Yes, there is a lot of chauvinistic jiggery-pokery in some NHS hospitals faced with a woman who, if she is kept in the queue for a few more weeks, will be unable to have a termination. But there are also Pregnancy Advisory services advertised in every city . . . The real barriers to women's free choice about motherhood conceal themselves behind difficulties of contraception and abortion because they are as complex, as far-reaching and as nebulous as were the barriers which stood between the first suffragettes and the vote.

Women are expected to want children. Those who have no permanent partnership with a man are widely assumed to be looking for one. Those who have such a partner and do not marry him are allowed to avoid children because they are still

53

single, but they are widely assumed to be working to persuade him to 'tie the knot'. Those who are actually married but nevertheless remain childless can take their pick between being thought to be making secret visits to an infertility clinic; having picked a man who refuses to have his sperm counted; or being, in some ill-defined way, 'extremely selfish'. A woman who actually admits to being married to a man with whom she is fertile but not intending to reproduce herself will face the spectre of the menopause dangled before her with cries of 'you'll be sorry when it's too late'. And how can she know whether she will be sorry or not? Free choice it may be but it does have a time limit. Under circumstances like these an abortion may seem like tempting some woman-hating fate. 'Supposing I get rid of this one because I don't want one now, and then later on I want one and I can't have any ...' We are conditioned to dread the menopause, just as we are taught to expect violent personal reactions to hysterectomies and sterilization procedures as well as to abortions. Some of us get them. How many of us need to is another matter.

All these attitudes and pressures seem to me legitimate targets for the women's movement which, because it largely ignores motherhood, has played little part in airing them or in helping women cope. Yet the right to choose, in consultation with her partner – even making that choice a factor in choice of partnership itself – is surely something every woman should have. The choice to remain childless, irrespective of sexual or marital status, is one which should be respected as no business of anyone outside that partnership. I do not acknowledge (even for myself one day) a right to grandchildren.

But if having a child is to become a positive and genuinely free and personal decision, rather than something most women just drift into because it is expected by and of them, they need information on which to make that decision.

At present the vast majority of first babies are born to people who have little idea what difference the birth is going to make to their lives. Sex education in school will have given them the biological facts of procreation and perhaps of preventing it, too. In a few schools, and all honour to them, some girls (perhaps even a few boys as well) will have studied 'mother-craft'; bathed a baby doll, visited a day nursery and perhaps helped at a playgroup. But while teaching of this kind heads in the right direction, it does not go nearly far enough. When we give 'career advice' to teenagers, we try to show them what life as an electronic engineer, a nurse, a salesperson or an apprentice carpenter will actually be *like*. Of course we talk about what they will earn to start with and what the promotion prospects are like, but we also try to give them a picture of what they will be doing with their time, who will be working alongside them, what their daily conditions will be like. We need to do the same kind of thing for motherhood or, better still, for parenthood as a whole.

People who have brought up children tend to assume that adolescents have a lingering picture in their minds of life with small children, stemming directly from their own childhoods. But most families now consist of only about two children, usually born within two to three years of each other. In such a family neither child will grow up with any recollection of how things were during their first years. Nor will either child retain a conscious image of his or her own mother's mothering behaviour. Few people can consistently recollect events which took place before they were four or five and many cannot go back that far. So an elder child's first 'family' images will probably contain a younger brother or sister of at least two or three, while a younger child's pictures will be of the parents with a primary school child. Of course there are still families in which a late last child gives a much older sister or brother some actual experience with babies; and there are others which have younger cousins around. But these are a minority. It is perfectly possible to grow up in Britain today and reach sexual maturity without ever giving one conscious thought to the infants of your own species. Never has this been brought home to me more forcibly than when helping first-time mothers who want to breast-feed. Very few have ever before *seen* a baby put to the breast.

Once a woman is pregnant – when in terms of deciding

whether or not she wants to embark on being a mother, it is already too late – she will get a great deal of expert preparation. But the expertise is directed towards staying healthy while the baby is inside her and staying calm and helpful while it gets out. Most antenatal teaching – and there are honourable exceptions such as the classes run by the National Childbirth Trust – stops abruptly when the baby, washed and wrapped, is put into the mother's arms. No wonder that many women regard birth as an end in itself rather than as the beginning of something. No wonder that many women who are not yet pregnant consider having a baby in terms of what they think they would feel at that moment of greeting. No wonder that many first-time mothers are in a daze of amazed and exhausted bewilderment when they come for that six-week check-up. At the moment, women who become mothers have to find out the hard way what life as a mother is like. If they do not like what they find, it is too late to change their minds. Being a mother is not like sailing a boat or making a first hang-gliding trip. You cannot say to yourself, 'Well, I've got to survive today but I'll never do this again.' That mother is going to have to do it and go on doing it for weeks, months and years.

② So the second part of my mothers' liberation charter is *the right to full information about the job of being somebody's mother*. I do not mean either the bliss or the hell of motherhood. The bliss has to do with love, with the emotional rewards of being an immature and dependent person's completing half. Like other kinds of love it is individual and indescribable. I think we can leave it alone because most females have some kind of emotional/sentimental drive towards having/loving babies and they will therefore provide this aspect for themselves. The hell, if there is one, is individual and largely avoidable. There is usually more jealousy than educational intent behind those cries of, 'You won't be able to go out every night once baby comes, you know.'

What young people, especially girls, need to know is everything they can grasp about the development, physical, mental, social and emotional, of normal children. It is out of their necessary development that children's particular needs, at any given age/stage, spring. It is those needs, sequence after sequence, phase after phase, which responsible parents must strive to meet both for their child's sake and for their own. Most educators think it important that children should grow up with some picture of the development of our society. Few pupils escape 'The Romans' in history lessons or 'The Break with Rome' in Religious Knowledge. How strange that it is not thought equally desirable for children to grow up with some picture of their own development, as human beings. It is an easy option for teachers, too. I have yet to meet a group of children of any age and either sex who were not deeply fascinated by the subject once it was introduced. For confirmation, try 'How do you think children learn to talk?' on any ten-year-old you may have available.

I am confident that if every prospective mother had a clear understanding of the outline developmental needs of all children, almost every one would see, for herself, the pointlessness and the irresponsibility of producing a child without intending to do her damnedest to meet them. I am also confident that as she came to understand the needs, she would realize that they can only be met by an individual and long-term caretaker. Probably she would then take it for granted that if she was going to have a baby at all she herself would be its mother-figure, its caring-person, as well as its blood-mother. Her willingness to give what she had discovered that her child would need, would become, as it should be, the major factor in her decision about whether or not to become a mother.

Decisions, however carefully they have been made, can prove wrong or can be made wrong by circumstances. There would still be some mothers who found themselves unwilling or unable to mother their children. But, armed with the kind of information I am advocating, these would know that they had to find some other person, an alternative caring-figure, for them. Once you truly understand what is known of the developmental needs of young human beings, you can no longer accept group-care in infancy. You can no longer tell yourself that a nursery, run by experts and full of toys and space, is as good for your child as life with you, however inept you feel and however cramped and impoverished your quarters.

'Your baby needs you' sounds today like a cranky slogan but it contains a truth which every woman should know *before she has a child.* So the third part of my mothers' liberation charter is the *right to an understanding of her own importance to any child she has.*

Since this is an aspect of mothers' rights which is not simply ignored but subtly denied by the state, the women's movement and the media, I shall try to make its case.

Babies and Individual Care

I began by heading this section 'Why mothers matter'. But it does not, as far as we know, matter in the least to a baby whether he has his real mother or not. There is absolutely no magic in the blood-tie except in so far as it may predispose the person who is mothering to feel like doing it well. What does matter to the baby is that he should have someone who responds to him, and to whom he can respond, *as a mother.* He also needs a father-person and as many other intimately affectionate people, of both sexes and all ages, as his social group can provide. Meeting a baby's basic needs does not commit people to being Mr and Mrs Jones in a city flat with one other child. Those needs can be met in an infinite variety of social settings and may be a great deal easier to meet in a tribe than in the nuclear family which represents conventional family life in Britain. But whatever the setting, that personal mother-figure is central and the father-figure, who is personal both to the baby *and* the mother-figure, is vitally important. Here and now, these people will usually be the baby's parents and re-lations so, for easy prose, I shall refer to them as such. But the message is about mothering, not about giving birth. And it is about the feeling of group-belonging, not about conventional families.

New human beings are totally dependent on adults for survival and they remain dependent for longer than the young of any other mammal, even if allowance is made for differences in comparative life-spans. The new baby's helplessness is so complete that, in order to keep him alive at all, his mother must adapt her life totally to meeting his physical needs. It is not enough for her to have or to buy milk; even to leave her full breasts or a bottle dangling within his reach. When he is hungry she must stop whatever she is doing and positively feed him. It is not enough for her to pick him up when she wants to move somewhere. She must positively carry him. Unlike even our nearest relations, the apes, the new baby will neither help himself to available milk nor cling to maternal transport. His survival requires positive action from his mother.

But all species that have survived are programmed for survival rather than extinction so the human baby's helplessness is coupled with powerful weapons to ensure that the adult world does provide help. The earliest weapon is pointed at the blood-mother because it consists of a continuing symbiosis between mother and child which is felt physically by the mother even though she and the child are physically separate. If she is within sensing distance at all, the new baby's crying will have all kinds of physical effects on her body. A rush of blood to her breasts may remind her that they contain the baby's milk and serve as a clear signal to her to feed him. She may feel the uterine contractions women call 'after-pains' or she may just experience a general rush of adrenalin through her body which says 'do something'. Whatever form it takes, the effect of her baby's crying serves as a clear call to her to take action on his behalf.

The action the baby needs from his mother is something only he and she together can establish and, at the start, it is often a question of trial and error. But babies' needs are very simple, obvious and repetitive. Desperation over a newborn's crying; those frantic pleas of 'What shall I *do*?' are seldom what they seem. If neither food nor any other obvious physical discomfort is the immediate answer, then the obvious physical comfort of cuddling, rocking, walking, soon will be. A mother who has, and feels that she has, all the time in the world to devote to the baby, quickly finds this out and can cope calmly with each new crying episode. It is the mother who is 'supposed' to be cooking for six, listening to her partner's stories about his day or practising her Yoga, who gets frantic. She does not really mean 'What shall I do?' and well-meaning attempts to explain how she should offer milk, check nappies, deflect sunlight and so forth totally miss the point. She means 'How can I split myself between what I can feel that my baby needs and what everyone else needs of me and/or expects me to need for myself?'

A mother who can let herself (and is permitted to) listen to her body, watch her baby and handle him at the times and in the ways that keep both of them comfortable, discovers that he is miraculously responsive. She meets his needs, responds to his global and unfocused demands and maintains his uneasy equilibrium in this strange new world. The more she does so, the more she comes to feel herself to be a 'good mother'. Each time the baby sucks himself into a blissful trance, hot heavy head cradled by her waiting, purpose-built elbow, she becomes clearer that this baby is something she can do, and do well. Each time he stops crying as she picks him up; each time those great blue eyes focus blearily on hers, she feels that he is acknowledging *her*. He is not. New babies know nothing of individual people; they neither know one from another nor themselves from anyone else. But their survival depends upon adult human beings so they are geared to pay attention to any who come within range. If there is a human face to look at, the baby will examine that rather than anything else. A human voice interests him more and soothes him faster than any other sound. The soft wrappings and rocking cradles, the cosy carrycots and canvas slings so beloved of western mothers work only because they mimic, or provide, the sensations of being held and carried by a person. So the people who care for new babies are *supposed* to take those babies' contented reactions personally. The baby reacts in that way both because he is content with what has been done for him and because the signs of his contentment act as a reward to the mother-person and thus ensure that she will do it all over again next time he is in need. The reward system breaks down, of course, if it is never the same person who is in charge on successive occasions. The fact that you tipped the dustmen last week will not affect the service you get today if the vehicle is manned by different dustmen.

Somewhere around four to six weeks after birth – at just about the time when the mother's body is returning to her pre-pregnant norms and the *physical* symbiosis with her baby is wearing off – he produces a new way of making sure that his caretaker keeps on caring: smiling.

A baby's early smiles are an attention-producing alchemy of enchantment. They work as a euphoric on most mothers, bring the enormity of what they have done home to fathers who had gone back to thinking about other things, and cause even the most blasé of duty visitors to stay an extra five minutes hoping for one more glimpse. After the usual careful inspection from your hairline to your chin and back up to your eyes, the baby's face is transformed by a slow, intimate grin which looks as if it were meant only for you. If anything is needed to ensure that he gets picked up, cuddled, talked to, played with, that is it. Even jealous toddlers often have to acknowledge that this tiresome thing is 'getting a bit nice . . .'

Newly-smiling babies are still completely promiscuous with their favours. Their smiles feel like adequate reward for broken nights and long, confusing days, but they will be produced for anyone and everyone, even for those who have never offered anything but this one contact. But the baby who is ready to smile at people-in-general is ready to begin the most intensive stage in the lifelong process of learning about people-in-particular. Over a period of six or seven months he is going to develop from being interested in everyone to being passionately devoted to those selected individuals who relate intimately to him. Only when he can differentiate the important people in his environment from 'others', and from each other, can he begin to learn about and interact with them as individuals.

So, using all his five senses and a widening range of increasingly subtle cues, the baby embarks on the first sorting out of his 'special' people which is a vital part of his apprenticeship to humanity. If he is lucky, the 'special' people are right there for him to consider, going on caring for him just as they have done since he was born. But if he is less fortunate, those first smiles, which are such an important indicator of the absolute necessity for stable individual care, will coincide with radical changes in the people around him. If he is to go to a long-term foster home or for adoption, he will probably go just about now. It is late for his blood-mother, who must endure the separation after being exposed to weeks of his 'care-for-me' tactics. It is late for the new mother-figure who has missed those tactics. And it is late for the baby whose work has been wasted. If he comes from that tiny but continuing minority of families whose wealth equates a baby with a monthly nurse, she will probably leave the family just about now. If his mother always intended to go back to work at the earliest possible moment, this is about the time when her doctor will consider letting her do so. If he is to go to a residential or a day nursery, this is likely to be the first age-point at which he can be accepted.

A baby who is cared for by one person almost all the time will quickly learn to distinguish her from everyone else and he will show that he has done so by behaving differently with her.

A baby who is cared for by two or more people will take rather longer to sort them out but, *provided they are always the same people*, he will soon learn to distinguish them both from each other and from 'outsiders'.

Patterns of multiple-care vary widely, but it is rare in this country for a baby to have more than one person equally available all the time. We simply do not know whether a baby who was offered such a wealth of personal attention would select one person for his primary attachment or would attach himself equally to all. There are indications, from highly technical studies, that this very young age-group pays more attention to female faces and voice-tones than to male, when offered both in an experimental situation. But whether a baby whose mother and father both answered every cry would actually engineer more attention from mother than from father, we do not know.

Where both parents do share the care of a young baby, mothers tend to slip into primary place, with fathers being content both to give and receive something which is better described as different, than less.

Whether a second caretaker is father, grandmother, nanny, mother's help or day-minder, the essence of the arrangement is usually that he or she takes turns with the mother. A baby in this age-stage will almost always accept them equally. He is learning to distinguish people as a necessary preliminary to loving. So vociferous assertions of preference usually come much later.

The kind of multiple-care which a baby is likely to receive in any kind of institutional group is a very different matter. Staff in charge of some of the best residential and day nurseries in the country have lavished ingenuity, devotion and all the money they could get on trying to provide stability of care for the babies in their charge. It cannot be done. The institution does not only have babies to cope with, it also has staff. Their training, rotation-for-experience, promotion, holidays and sickness produce an ever-changing array of caretakers. The baby will make no objection because he does not yet know one from another, but his learning of one from another may be delayed if there is no 'special' one who lasts. In extreme instances, babies who were cared for in institutions from very early on have grown into childhood still with the emotional promiscuity appropriate to only the first weeks of life. It is as if the lack of anyone 'special' had kept them at the stage of being interested in everyone but loving no one, indefinitely.

Once a baby 'knows' his special person or people, the process of becoming attached, of human emotional apprenticeship, can begin. He continues to need physical care, of course, but for full development as a person he needs social, emotional and intellectual care, too. In a satisfactorily affectionate, caring relationship he gets all these things mixed up together and nobody has anything to gain from trying to sort them out. The little islands of 'playtime' slotted into the babycare manuals amidst the feeding and dressing, the washing and health care which otherwise fill them, are meaningless. The baby is cuddled while he feeds, tickled while he is dressed, swooshed up and down his bath, carried from place to place and smiled at and talked to all through. But while there is no point in an individual mother who is reasonably content with her role trying to work out what kind of care she is giving her baby, there is a point in understanding that the social aspects of the relationship are actually more important to the baby than the physical ones. It is widely assumed that the 'love' which babies develop for their mothers is some kind of cupboard love. The baby cries and is picked up and held for a feed. Afterwards he smiles and seems content. The feed made him happy? Yes, but the smiles and the pleasure are not for the milk, which has vanished inside him, but for the person who gave him affectionate attention. If someone else had fed him with a bottle at detached arm's length and then handed him to his mother to be held, it would not be the milk-provider who received his smiles, it would be the mother. Not many years ago, babies in Israeli kibbutzim were communally cared for by trained nurses while their mothers did a full day's work and had a full night's sleep. For two hours each evening the babies visited their parents who had nothing to do during that time but pay them affectionate attention. Only two hours out of twenty-four; no feeds, no relief from discomfort; just social talk and play, but it was not the nurses those babies came to love: it was the parents.

The baby focuses on his special people and with and through them he learns. He learns about people, by watching and listening to their behaviour. He learns about emotion, by experiencing his and theirs and their reactions to both. He learns the world he shares with them by watching them in it and examining the little pieces of it which they bring for him to play with. Above all, he learns about himself as a positive and effective force in his small environment. Bit by bit he learns the reiterated and vital message: 'If I do this, that happens . . .' He receives care, but he is never a passive recipient. His mother's behaviour affects him, but his affects her just as much and therefore affects what she does with and for him. He smiles and coos because she smiles and talks to him. But she smiles and talks some more because he is smiling and cooing. He plays just as much part in shaping his own environment and his care-takers' lives as they do in shaping his for him.

This kind of interaction, this endless cycle of action-effect-more action-further effect, working both from caretaker to baby and from baby to caretaker, is the essence of creative babycare. Because it *is* interactive, it is absolutely dependent on the baby's having always the same person or people around.

In the interests of him turning into a recognizably human being, we want the baby to notice that everything he does has an effect and we want him gradually to grasp the range of effects which he has. He can only do this at optimum speed if the people he is affecting are always the same; only then will the range of responses his actions evoke be sufficiently internally consistent to be comprehensible and repeatable. And for the baby, as for anybody else, learning is impossible without under-standing and repetition. Try remembering a simple telephone number in Chinese when you've been told it once and you will see what I mean.

As well as noticing the effects of his actions, we also want the baby to take increasingly mature and subtle actions into his repertoire. Early on, when he needs something, he will cry until it is produced, the need dies down or he is distracted into forget-ting it. But crying until something happens is a very basic level of communicative action and not one which we want our new people kept at for long. The baby must learn that facial ex-pressions, hand and body gestures, sounds and, eventually, words are also effective. This kind of learning depends on being with people who 'know' and 'understand' him, because it is only their *re*action to his new (and perhaps initially random) action which will tell him to try it again. A mother knows her baby's face so well that when he reaches a point where particular lip-quivering things happen to it just before he cries she will cer-tainly notice. Eventually there will come a time when she reacts to that expression, instead of waiting for the cry and the baby notices that she has done so. In the same way, she knows the baby's hand gestures and the objects he plays with. The two pieces of information together lead to the day when the wildly-flailing arms that are part of 'I want', lead her to the object he actually wanted. Neither of them will ever know how much of the sequence was deliberate, nor how many times before she had responded similarly to a similar gesture but picked the 'wrong' object. All that will matter is that the baby has got what he wanted by a new, repeatable and comparatively soph-isticated method. She knows his voice, too, and since most of the deliberate sounds he utters are precursors of speech and speech is probably the most vital accomplishment in his hu-manity, her knowledge is important. If you do not know a baby well enough to differentiate between the 'Uh-uh-uh' of 'I want' and the 'Uuh-nuu-nuu' of 'I'm tired', you cannot contribute to his early language development.

A baby who does not have anybody special, but is cared for by many well-meaning strangers in turn, or one who is cared for sketchily and without concentration, sharing his caretaker with other needful small people, is like an adult who moves from country to country, knowing the language of none. Baby and adult must each rely on the universal language of gross gesture and tolerate high levels of isolation and low levels of under-standing. Neither can develop any subtlety of communication nor certainty as to whether or why things have been understood or have taken place. The adult returns home with relief. The baby had better stay there.

Many babies start life with the special people who are usually their parents but then, when emotional attachment, feelings of effectiveness and communication have begun to develop, find themselves with strangers. Depending on his age and maturity and his previous experiences, such a baby will have developed a wide range of more or less subtle cues and he will be beginning to have expectations about people's responses to them. Having those cues missed or misinterpreted, or receiving responses which are new to him or out of line with anything he knows, will shake his confidence. But he is still a survivor. If the strangers are part- or full-time substitute parents who, once on the scene, remain constantly part of his life, he will gradually adapt. If his mother is around to help him make the transition, to 'translate him' for the newcomers and to blend their 'style' with her own, he will adapt more quickly. The new people will be made 'special'. He will teach them to understand him and to respond to him just as he taught his mother. But if the newcomers to his life have no time to 'listen' to him, concentrate on him, feel their way with him, perhaps because he is now part of a group or perhaps because they are part of a stream of short-term caretakers, his development may truly suffer.

I do not think that it is possible to over-emphasize these twin factors of individuality and continuity in a baby's care. Except in extreme cases — as of physical cruelty, dangerous neglect or the total maternal withdrawal that sometimes comes with mental illness — they override every other feature distinguishing 'good' from 'bad'. I was made very aware of it when recently a friend brought me her four-month baby for the day while she attended a distant family funeral. 'I shan't worry about her with you,' she said. 'In fact I just hope she won't realize what an inept mother I am after a day in your expert hands . . .' A meant-to-be-flattering joke, but with a slight ring of truth to it all the same. She *was* insecure about her mothering; she was trying to convince herself that the baby would be just as well off with some 'motherly type' if she soon went back to outside work. She did, just a little bit, feel that the baby might have a better day in my charge than in her own. The baby and I got on fine but again and again I was flummoxed as to the exact meaning of her cues. Settled for a sleep after her lunch, she whimpered. What did she mean? Did she not want to sleep? Did she need wrapping more closely to help her relax? Had she not sucked enough to be comfortably full? Had she got a bellyful of air? Did she need the stimulus of my presence removed so that she could let go of the world? Some knowledge of babies enabled me to list to myself tens of possible messages. But only personal knowledge of *this* baby would have enabled me to pick the right one and respond appropriately. We had to use trial and

error and it all worked out. But trial and error reactions from
'their' adults, to messages about their basic needs, are something
babies have a right to get over with in their very first weeks
when they are making themselves clear to their parents. Had
this baby and I been set for a permanent, if late-starting, relationship, no doubt we should have come to terms with each
other over time. As strangers, no amount of expertise from me
could balance out the familiarity of her mother. Spending the
day with me certainly did her no harm because she had spent
the day before, and would spend the day after, at home. Tiny
gaps in a long-term fabric of blanket-care cannot damage a
process as long and close-knit as human development. So a
'special' person does not have to be there for her child every
minute of every twenty-four hours. But big gaps can do
damage. Three days of every week spent not always with me
but with each of several people like me, or with only a small
share in somebody looking after others like her, and that baby
would have had to alter course. So a 'special person' who is not
going to be there *most* of the time had better find somebody
who will be when she is not.

People who reckon to be 'good with babies' sometimes feel
that a particular mother is so insensitive to her baby's cues
(which they themselves can clearly see even if they cannot interpret them) that almost anyone would be 'better for him'.
Mothers, and other caretakers, do of course vary in their sensitivity just as babies vary in the clarity and emphasis with which
they communicate and react. Temperamental matching and
mismatching of this kind can make it unfairly much easier for
one mother-child pair to mesh smoothly together than for the
next pair to do so. A cued-in mother with a baby who gives
clear signals and emphatic reactions, can hardly fail to make a
good pair. But put the same mother with a less focused baby or
the same baby with a less sensitive mother and the whole thing
becomes more difficult.

But, within the limits of ordinarily decent behaviour, such
judgements about a mother's child-care are almost always
wrong because they ignore the interactive nature of the re-

lationship between mother and child. A mother who is not very tuned-in to her baby will be consistent in her lack of reactivity. Because she is consistent, because her behaviour is a part of what she is, her baby will both adapt himself to her and teach her to adapt herself to him. If he can only get attention by going right through from quivering lip to whimpers to full-fledged yells, he will learn to yell fast and loud. Because these yells penetrate even her consciousness, his mother will come to recognize them at, say, half-pitch. Between the baby learning to give stronger cues and the mother learning to notice milder ones, the two of them will eventually meet in the middle, somewhere around half-time and half-volume. If the critic believes that babies should not have to cry at all in order to get what they want and need, it is easy to ignore these adaptations and to see that baby as a victim. But provided he has his mother's basic goodwill and she has her sanity, he is not a victim but a partner in the creation of his environment. He is making it in collaboration with his mother and between the two of them the result is almost certainly 'good enough' mothering for him, even if it falls, as we all fall, far below somebody's ideal.

Having learned a good deal about his effect on other people as well as about theirs on him, a baby in the second-half of his first year normally develops a positive passion for one particular caretaker, usually his mother. Through his relationship with her he is going to discover, feel and practise emotions which are, as far as we can tell, both as strong and as various as the emotions of older people. He is going to love and depend totally on her, using her as his mirror for himself and the world. Almost everything which happens to him will reach him through mother-filters as he buries his head in her shoulder to muffle that too-loud bang, and looks at her face to see by her expression whether this approaching stranger is friend or foe.

By this stage there is no need for any outsider to state the baby's need for one constant figure to be attached to. The baby himself makes it loudly obvious. He loves her and he wants her; he wants her whenever he is awake which is for as many hours as he can manage, and for perfection he wants her full attention directed towards him. Of course he cannot always have constant or undivided attention. Mothers have other things to do and other people who are important to them and it is right, for the baby as well as for themselves, that this should be so. He will experience the jealousy and the rage which are part of human loving. But he will also learn that mother does not belong entirely to him – which is an important piece of reality – and that she is a loving and lovable person to others as well as himself. He will also gradually discover that he can have fun sharing mother from time to time and that the people he has to share her with have something to offer him too.

But not having mother all to himself all the time is a very different matter from not having her around. This he does need and should have. His relationship with her stands as a prototype for all his later love-relationships. The more he can be allowed to indulge it now, the more loving and receptive of love he will be later. There is even evidence that he is likely to repeat with his own children the long-forgotten emotional experiences he has during this phase, a loved and loving baby being able to love and tolerate his own children's demands in a way which a love-rationed child can never do. It may be here, in love rather than in circumstance, that much of that 'cycle of deprivation' has its roots.

If love now breeds easy loving later, accepted dependence now breeds independence later. A baby of eight, nine or ten months often seeks almost continual help, comfort and reassurance from his mother. The more he is helped to feel that she is indeed there for him and ready to support him whenever he feels the need, the more independent of her he will be able to be when he is older. It is as if consistently meeting his needs to be dependent built him a dependable platform on which to stand, one day, on his own two feet.

Some mothers find this period of being intensely and openly loved and needed, highly enjoyable and good for their egos. Most of us like to be liked and find it easier to approve of ourselves when those around us clearly do so. But others, usually those who have found the baby emotionally draining during the early months, find that they are now being loved more than they can easily stand. They may try to ration themselves; deliberately holding back from the baby, often telling themselves, as they detach the clinging arms and put the weeping baby in a playpen, that he is getting 'spoiled'. Research has sounded a warning note for such mothers. Pairs of mothers and babies were closely observed and wide variations between the pairs were found in the amount of social interaction which went on within them. But the variation was all in the mothers' behaviour; none of it was in the babies'. *All* the babies made frequent social advances to their mothers and invariably reacted with pleasure to any made by her. The mothers who often ignored their babies and seldom initiated contact with them were the ones who said that they found child-care boring.

So the baby needs that warm, continuous, stimulating and personal relationship and he puts a great deal into it himself, with smiles and sounds, with excitement and busy contentment. Where a mother notices, enjoys and encourages it, the old circle of pleasant interaction is complete and ongoing. But where she refuses, or is unable, to interact, a vicious circle tends to form with the baby asking more and more and the mother giving less and less. Mothers need to understand, for their own as well as for their children's sakes, that a baby who seeks attention and gets it will stop looking for it until he needs, or is pleased to be offered, some more. But a baby who seeks attention and is told 'to get on with it' will go on and on, because he must. It is not too much attention which produces the whiney babies people label 'spoiled'; it is too little attention too reluctantly given. What is spoiled is the natural course of the baby's development and his mother's nerves.

Vicious circles are easier to avoid than they are to climb out of. I believe that if every woman was prepared for this stage in her baby's development and was helped to anticipate it as necessary to him and a bouquet to her as a mother, many more would skirt the edges of the whirlpool. Sadly, onlookers, even the 'expert' ones who should know better, tend to confuse loving with spoiling and legitimate needs with unreasonable demands. We have no fun-ethic where mothers and babies are concerned. A bored baby is boring, but how often do we take the simple path of entertaining him so that he stops being bored and boring us? No, we go dutifully on with the ironing, managing each shirt less well as the grumbles increase in volume and persistence. When a nine-month baby cries because his mother leaves the room, the visiting health visitor does not say admiringly 'He certainly is mad about you now, isn't he?' No, she says 'you're letting him get spoiled you know ... making a rod for your own back.'

I believe that a pleasantly enjoyable time for all concerned is what really matters because pleasure and happiness have their own momentum and it is within them that people, young or old, learn and function best. But our puritanism makes such attitudes seem unacceptably hedonistic. We are more concerned with 'good babies' and 'good mothers' than we are with happy ones. And look at our definitions of infant and maternal goodness: a good baby, in most circles, is a quiet and undemanding one. But who is he good *for*? Certainly not for himself since it is through demanding and receiving attention that he will develop and learn. A good mother, in at least some circles, is one who minces liver and fresh vegetables for her baby's lunch. But who is she good for? Not for the baby, who cares not a jot if his lunch comes out of a can and who would much rather have her time than her cooking. And not for herself, since mincing liver is a revolting business and almost everyone can think of something they would rather do.

Toddlers and Individual Care

Nothing is sudden in human development, nor does anything have a fixed age of occurrence or duration. Nevertheless every new person eventually reaches a point where the term 'baby' no longer seems to fit him although, when you look at a schoolchild, 'child' does not seem quite right either. So I split the period between, say, the first birthday and the start of compulsory full-time schooling into two phases. The first I call 'toddlers' and the second 'pre-school children'. I suppose a toddler officially becomes a toddler when he starts to toddle on his own two feet. But, as we shall see, being a toddler is largely a state of mind and emotion, so any individual child may become one earlier or later. When a toddler becomes a pre-school child I do not know without meeting him. It has something to do with increasing length and less protruding belly. It has a lot to do with emotional independence and the extent to which the child has got it all together. But perhaps it has most to do with speech: with the kind of easy verbal communication which enables the adult world to give and to receive reasons, explanations and apologies, unsupported by physical action. When you stop thinking of your child as a toddler is up to you and to him. For the purposes of my argument an arbitrary two-and-a-half to three will do.

Toddlers need individual care just as much as babies do. But unfortunately for all concerned they can be extremely misleading about it. A young baby is obviously totally dependent on *somebody*; an older baby spends a lot of his time vociferously asserting his inability to manage for a moment without one person in particular; but a toddler is different. He has learned that, like it or not, he is a separate being from his mother or anybody else and he has reached the stage when he has to begin to act like one. In doing so, he can be bolshy, rude, violent, rejecting, ungrateful, uncaring, cheeky, bossy . . . name it and it is bound to fit.

Mothers who are complaining about their toddlers often put all the upset which they feel down to *behaviour*; to the mess, muddle and trouble the toddler creates. But an honest mother who has truly learned to acknowledge her child as a person, will admit that the real trouble is that he hurts her feelings. Just as some adults find it curiously shameful to apologize to a child they have wronged, so many find it shameful to admit that anyone so small could actually damage their *amour propre*. But it is no shame. That toddler is another person; his ability to hurt other people is part of his humanity and his mother's liability to it is an important area of learning for him.

Everyone who has ever had dealings with a toddler will recognize as typical the sudden, almost random, assertions of autonomy and independence which usually take the form of screams of 'No!', 'Go 'way' and 'Me do it . . .' Few recognize the existence or the nature of the conflict which the toddler's outbursts reflect. People accept that 'he's got to that difficult age . . .' without asking themselves why it has to be so difficult: why the toddler cannot be polite and cooperative in his search for independence.

The simplified answer is that the toddler has arrived at a double-bind. He has reached that point in his overall development where further growth demands that he start to become independent and autonomous. Yet becoming so is acutely worrying for him because every clash with mother, every pitting of his new young will against long-accepted authority, threatens the love aspect of the relationship on which he is still entirely dependent. The developmental imperative of independence is in conflict with the emotional imperative of love. The result is a muddle.

Veering wildly between the two, the toddler's behaviour is as contradictory as it is irrational. One moment he demands that his mother 'Go 'way', but the next moment he is weeping because she has done so. One moment he insists that 'Me do it', the next he delivers bitter reproaches to his mother for not helping him. The big boy with a gun becomes the baby with a bottle; the affectionate playmate becomes the one who hates you. But the veering is like a pendulum: if it is allowed its swing it will eventually settle into the middle of its own accord. The toddler who is tolerated slowly learns the vital lesson which will free him to become a pre-school child. He learns that independence and loving protection are not alternatives; he learns that he can have the best of both extremes, obey both those imperatives. He can be an independent person who is loved and loving; an autonomous person who is still protected.

Since the internal conflict is about his newly-aware self in relation to the 'special' person to whom he is attached, it follows that the toddler can only fully learn this lesson if he is allowed to experiment with that relationship almost continuously. When the toddler sets off across the park, he adventures *from* mother. When he throws a tantrum, he rages *at* mother. When he croons and strokes and cuddles, he does so *to* mother. And when he weeps in desolation, he does so *for* mother. She is the centre. The toddler is testing his relationship with his mother for safety and for flexibility, asking, so to speak, 'Do you love me whatever I do? Will you always be there however much I let myself grow up? If I go away for a bit will I be able to find you again? Do you go on loving me even when, for the moment, I do not love you?' He has to love and to hate *one and the same person* and to discover that both extremes of emotion are safe because his basic relationship stays securely in the middle. He needs proof both of his lovability and of his lovingness and there are no short cuts to providing it. The toddler's mother has to go on (and on, and on) showing that however much she dislikes some of the things he *does*, nothing shakes her love for the person he *is*.

But this kind of steadiness at the centre of unsteady emotions is a great deal easier to prescribe than it is to provide. Mothers have to be mature and self-confident within themselves if they are to tolerate their toddlers' hating-moments and destructiveness while remaining warm to the loving and creative ones. Understanding what is really going on helps. But if a woman's self-esteem as a mother has been low from the beginning, it may well ebb below her level of tolerance when her child becomes a 'terrible two'. The obvious dependency of the baby has gone, now that the child walks and talks, looks and plays, like a child. The obvious, continuous and passionate love has gone, too, except when the toddler reveals it in flashes through his bravado. He is generally tough and active, he often seems bored with what his mother can provide for him to do and for much of the time he seems cross with her and with his life. It is not surprising that many mothers genuinely believe that their toddlers need a radical change. It is not surprising that many are thankful to seek a partial parting of the ways. Playgroup leaders and nursery class teachers are all familiar with the knell-of-doom phrases with which such mothers plead for group-admission for their child:

We both need a break.
He's much better with other people.
He's bored just with me, he needs other children.
He won't do anything I say; I've spoiled him; he needs the corners knocked off.

Many toddlers are already in some form of group-care, part- or full-time, and if bureaucracy ever puts institutions where its red tape is, thousands more will be. I neither believe that group-admission is right for the toddlers or the groups they are admitted to, nor that this is the only solution for their mothers. Solutions must wait for another chapter, but I will try now to state the case against groups for toddlers.

No form of group-care is appropriate for toddlers although the degree of inappropriateness will vary with the wide variation in types of group. Attendance at a playgroup on two afternoons each week, with mother present, or sometimes present and always involved, is most unlikely to do the toddler any harm. At the other extreme, full-day attendance at a day nursery, with mother excluded by her own outside job and/or by professional staff, is likely to do him considerable harm. The arguments against group-care therefore apply to all groups but apply with increasing force as groups take children further from their mothers for longer periods.

Toddlers turn into pre-school children and *when they do*, some forms of group experience become highly appropriate for many of them. The job which an ongoing group can do for children who *are* ready to attend is made far more difficult by the inclusion of children who are not. So if groups are not good for toddlers, neither are toddlers good for groups. In presenting the arguments against their admission, I shall deal with both these strands as they happen: together.

Toddlers starting at groups are likely to see their mothers' arrangements for them to attend as partial rejection. The child who does not see it that way at first – because mother stays with him, describes it as 'his' group and helps him enjoy the new toys and so forth – will come to see it that way the first time he does not feel like going and she makes him. Cleaning your teeth can be fun, but it does not take a child long to learn that fun is a by-product and that he has to do it whether he likes it or not because it is 'good for him'. Group-attendance enters the same category the moment mother says 'you must'.

At the group, a toddler whose mother stays with him may survive well, just as he survives tea parties and trips to big stores. There are a lot of people around but his focus, mother, is there, so he can largely ignore them. And he will. There will be a little mother–child island in the midst of the group and, like any other island, it will divert the tides of group-activity and communication, just a little. If the mother tries to prevent this, by joining in as the mothers of older children participating in a playgroup join in, storms will instantly blow up. The toddler is not ready to share his mother's attention with strange children and he hates her to get involved with strange adults. He will fight to keep her to himself and if he cannot he will want to leave.

If and when the toddler's mother leaves him at the group, she leaves him without a focus. There is a play-leader, nursery teacher or nurse, but he is not ready to be led in play or in learning or to be physically cared for by anyone unfamiliar. His reaction will depend on his personality, previous experience and current relationship with that mother. He may hold himself aloof from the new adult; disregarding her, face averted, until mother returns. He may reject her with fury because she is the only person available to fill mother's role and she is not mother. Or he may try to use her, that only available person, as a mother-surrogate.

Occasionally a play-leader, or other adult in charge of a group, is so touched by a toddler's willingness to use her as a mother-person that she loses sight of the strain which it imposes on her relationships within the group as a whole. The toddler asks for her support, asks to be loved, probably asks to be held and touched a great deal. Meeting these needs is enjoyable and being asked for them is flattering. The toddler is calm so where is the harm? The harm comes later. If the toddler is truly able to use the new adult as an alternative to his mother during group-hours, then the honeymoon of gentle dependency will not last for long, nor should it. He is not at a compliant/dependent age, so this touching behaviour clearly demonstrates the anxiety mother's desertion has caused in him. As soon as he feels secure in the new relationship, he will begin to exercise upon the mother-surrogate exactly the same trials which he puts his mother through. Her love will be challenged, stretched, examined for cracks and limits just as mother's is. If that adult is to go on doing well by him she will not have much left to offer to the other children. He has adopted her as a mother-substitute, just as he would adopt a child-minder or a nanny who was offered him instead of mother. He has forced her to be his 'special' person and in doing so he deprives the other children.

Although the group exists both of and for children, the toddler will find no magic in their company to lure him away from the adult. He is interested in watching them, he sometimes copies what they do, doing the same thing in parallel, but he does not need and cannot use them as companions yet. Adults are still primary. He is engaged in discovering himself as an independently functioning person who can nevertheless remain secure with his mother. Until he has done so he will not be able to abandon his preoccupation with adult love, protection and control and join a child's world. In the meantime, the play-tasks which are appropriate for him are either solitary or so skilled as to demand an adult partner.

The toddler has already learned a great deal about the world and its objects. His task now is to discover the basic natural laws which govern that world and the resulting rules for the behaviour of objects. Until he has done so, he will not be ready for intricate experimental and imaginative play which is appropriate for children at the next stage of intellectual development. He must learn the 'natural order' before he can impose himself upon it and try to change things. Gravity is a good example. He was born into earth-gravity and has had repeated experiences of its effects upon his body ever since. But before he can use his knowledge of gravity's effects, he must discover them in an ever-widening set of circumstances. Only once he knows, deep-down inside himself, that a dropped object will always fall *down* and will never, for reasons he will not understand for many years, go *up*, can he learn to play a sociable game with a ball, share other children's amazed pleasure in the behaviour of a kite, or comprehend the make-believe of being thistledown or an elephant. Even when he does first become ready to try a game of ball, he will not be able to play with another small child because each will throw so wildly that neither will ever get a reasonable shot. He will need a skilful adult to throw or roll the ball for him.

Children who have made basic concepts like gravity, volume, weight or velocity part of themselves find it impossible to allow for the apparent idiocy of those who have not. There is an enormous divide of understanding between most toddlers and most pre-school children, even though it is blurred by the vary-ing ages at which different children reach different stages. The two-year-old cannot understand the three-year-old's games but she can neither understand his difficulty nor muster any patience with it. 'It's down there, stupid,' she says crossly to the poor toddler who is gazing into the air for the ball he last saw shoot-ing skywards.

The divide is increased by difficulties in communication. While the language facility of young children is enormously variable and dependent on an enormous number of variables, inability to understand each other is widespread. Early in speech, children seem to tune their understanding almost exclu-sively to the channel of 'mother and other familiars'. Words and phrases which they understand and respond to from these select few are simply disregarded if they come from strangers, hence the phenomenon of the interpreter-mother who passes on to her toddler the friendly remarks of shopkeepers and other acquaint-ances. As the child matures, the 'reception-band' widens until it includes most adults who will address themselves directly to him and say something interesting. But for months longer it still excludes other small children. A sociable four-year-old asks the young newcomer his name. The newcomer does not even look at him. Irritated, the questioner repeats his question but still gets no reaction. At last an adult intervenes saying: 'This is John and he wants to know your name.' As if the adult had translated the message from a foreign tongue, the toddler answers. But just like those speakers at international conferences, he aims his reply at the adult-interpreter rather than at the originator.

It is in the vital area of language development that the two-way damage done by groups to toddlers, but also by toddlers to groups, is often most clearly seen. The toddler's language will not progress as fast as it could (and therefore should) if he is expected to manage without constant adult conversation. All those language exercises, like 'news-time' and 'story-time', will go straight over his head. He cannot listen to another child's talk. But it is also wrong for more mature children to have their still-recent skill in verbal communication rejected in this way. 'Why won't he listen to *me*?' says the offended four-year-old, while the child who is wanderingly recounting her adventures of yesterday to the group is all too aware that the toddler is not 'paying attention'.

A group is, or to be positively useful to children should be, a place for social interaction and play. But social play is a real effort to almost every small child and it is an effort which the one who is still a toddler will not, cannot and should not make.

He will not make the effort because there is no point for him in doing so yet. He does not need other children for satisfactory play and therefore he has no motive for trying to see how to make group-play work.

He cannot because he is not yet able to look at himself in relation to his peers, see himself through their eyes or put himself in their shoes. His mind is still on himself and, as a subsidiary part of self-discovery, on his mother or her substitute.

He should not because demands which are developmentally inappropriate for a child are never desirable even though they are sometimes necessary. Putting a toddler into a social group-situation is a little like putting a thirteen-year-old in charge of her brothers and sisters because her mother leaves or dies. She may cope; she may manage. She will almost certainly mature into some kind of human being. But nobody would suggest that such responsibilities and preoccupations are likely to be positively good for her development, or that her eventual splendidness means that other adolescents should be similarly treated.

Casual comparison of toddler and pre-school play reveals many of the developments which will have to take place in the younger children before they *are* ready, willing and able to play sociably with those who are more mature. More and more of a toddler's play has got to become imaginative. A toddler does not need another child to help him discover how much sand will fill his bucket or whether he can carry it when it is full. But once he wants to feed sand to a doll family, he begins to have a place for other children: to fill all the game's roles.

His play has to become more creative. He does not need (and cannot allow) a 'friend' to help him ride that trike. But once he wants to make it a garage out of cardboard boxes, he discovers that two may succeed where one fails or at least that the job goes faster if several cooperate.

Physical – and especially manual – skills and communication have to improve in parallel. Even if two children know that they want to play together, they cannot do so satisfactorily until they are adept enough to carry out their ideas, as well as being able to communicate them to each other. Two toddlers will ruin and undo each other's actions. No harm is meant. One has simply not understood that this teddy has been carefully bedded on that cushion which should not therefore be snatched up for use as a stool. The other has had a go at laying the 'table' the stool was to be drawn up to; it is just bad luck and toddler-coordination that has turned it from a cardboard-box-table into a cardboard squash.

Impulse control is a phrase used only with reference to toddlers and to the mentally disturbed. It denotes 'self-control' but covers people who have to control not just complete socialized selves but the raw and violent feelings and actions which lurk underneath. Toddlers cannot. Before they can be accepted for sociable play by other children, they have to learn to ask before they scream; scold before they wallop; look for ill-motivation before they 'kick back'; wait their turns, share, listen, and generally cooperate. It comes slowly to most children and remains precarious even in many of those who are ready to benefit from, and contribute to, group-life. But it can actually be delayed if a child is forced to accept superficially sociable relationships with other children before he is ready. The acute frustrations of those wildly thrown balls, unanswered questions, squashed boxes, misunderstood 'plans', flattened sand-pies and trampled toes are very hard to bear if the child is getting nothing out of the group to make them all worthwhile.

A skilful, interested and sensitive adult can do a great deal to oil the wheels of early social play and to keep things enjoyable for toddlers who are playing in parallel or watching those who are older. But while pre-school groups have a big role to play in demonstrating and emphasizing the value of socialized play-behaviour, they cannot do this until the children are all basically ready to learn. Nor should they try. Social development is, or should be, all of a piece with every other aspect of development.

Many people would argue that while all of the foregoing is, or may be, true, toddlers who are actually committed to group-care soon grow out of being toddlers and therefore become socialized more quickly than they would have done at home. 'The others will lick him into shape and he'll learn by imitating them . . .' People who take this line are usually those who very much want to believe that group-care is acceptable for the very young and who therefore use the observable fact that they do survive and develop, one way or another, as evidence to support it. So go back to that thirteen-year-old who finds herself in charge of the family. She too will adapt. She too will learn 'how to behave', will find ways of managing and will, after a fashion, develop. Does that prove that such responsibilities are good for her? That these are the optimum conditions for adolescent development and a useful way of short-circuiting its normally tumultuous path? No, of course not. Nobody would argue that, because nobody has any stake in thirteen-year-olds running families. But it is the same argument. Just as it is more appropriate for that girl to acquire maternal and household responsibilities out of mature sexuality rather than tragic deprivation, so it is better for the toddler to acquire socialized behaviour out of self-motivated maturity rather than sad necessity. If he is forced by a situation in which he has no choice, he will alter his *behaviour* without a concomitant alteration in his level of understanding, his stage in intellectual development. To be truly socialized, he has to be allowed to keep all these things advancing in step with each other. How he *behaves* is unimportant compared with what he *is*.

A look at even some aspects of the intellectual functioning and development of most children in their second and third years should make it clear that however successfully a group-behaviour ethos is imposed upon a toddler, that group cannot provide him with optimum learning conditions.

Toddler memory, for example, is still very immature. The things that he remembers are, if you think carefully about it, all things of which he has had repeated experience over a long period. He remembers his special people but not new acquaintances. He remembers the feel of the cuddly which guards him in bed but must open his eyes to find his new teddy. Anything which is new takes a long time to become implanted in his memory, while verbal exhortation or information, unbacked by physical experience, takes forever. He remembers-by-experience and at home the process happens so gradually that his family barely notices. But in a group his total inability to 'bear things in mind' is difficult to cope with – even dangerous. A shallow step between two rooms is a hazard which is new to him since he only recently started to walk. It lends itself to repeated experience as he trips and tumbles and, at home, his way to it can be barred when fatigue or illness reduce the competence of his coordination. But in a group? If the children are of mixed ages, access to the hazard cannot be blocked for the toddler without spoiling the environment for everyone else. If all are

83

toddlers there will always be somebody who is tired or unwell so one of the two rooms will have to be permanently blocked-off. Since toddlers cannot learn without repeated experience, none of them will ever learn about that blocked-off step . . .

Forethought is a kind of memory in reverse; people cannot think ahead until they can easily remember what happened last time and adapt their behaviour accordingly. The toddler cannot do this so, at home, his mother automatically does it for him. She knows that he will lock himself in the lavatory without pausing to think whether he can get out again. So she takes the lock off altogether or puts it high, out of his reach. She knows that he will climb that stepladder even though he will not be able safely to come down again, so she keeps it out of the way except when she can devote herself to supervising him. But in a group such easy and obvious adaptations to toddler minds cannot be made without offending or depriving others. At four, many children will want the privacy of a locked lavatory and all will need large-scale climbing equipment constantly available.

Both memory and forethought tie up with the ability to wait. Toddlers simply cannot. Anything that is wanted at all is wanted *now*, the moment it comes to mind. If you mention a story and put your hand to the book, the clamour will start immediately. Alone with a toddler his mother can quell the din and catch his attention by starting straight in. With practice she can read the first page while sitting herself down, gathering the toddler to her and settling him so that he can see the pictures. But in a group? Disaster. The story cannot be started for one without everyone else missing the beginning. Yet if the story does not start, toddlers will not stop fussing and so the impasse is complete. Reading aloud may never be as satisfactory a group-activity as *telling* stories, which allows both eye-contact and involving action. But with a toddler in a group of older children or in a group of all toddlers, it is virtually impossible.

Choices are difficult for toddlers, too. Offered one of two sweets, balloons or activities, the toddler will probably spin off into miserable indecision. He wants both and his attention is focused as much on the sadness of being deprived of one as on the pleasure of being given the other. Learning to choose is an important part of growing up; of that autonomy for which the toddler has to strive. But most choices are too complex and painful to be learning experiences. Faced with those two different sweets he must work out how he feels *now*: does he want a sweet? Introspection does not come easily to him. Then he must remember how he felt last time: did he like that kind of sweet? Unless they are of a long-familiar kind, his memory will probably let him down. Then he must foresee what he will feel in the immediate future. Will he enjoy eating the sweet . . .? One way or another he is going to make a lot of mistakes. Irritated adults will accuse him of 'keeping on changing his mind'; but in truth he has not been able to 'make up his mind' in the first place.

At home, in a one-to-one situation, he can be given choices which are tailored to help him learn by experience yet cause no agony. He can choose, for example, not which of two biscuits he will have, but which of the two biscuits he has already been given, he will eat first. He risks nothing because nobody is going to remove the one he allocates to second place. And he can 'change his mind' six increasingly crumby times if he needs to. 'One for each hand' is a time-honoured tradition in millions of families and a very appropriate one too.

But in a group designed to benefit children who are *ready* to be in a group, toddlers either have to be given no choices at all, being handled directively in everything, or their painful indecision will upset everyone. For these more mature children, choices of activity and companionship are important in helping them to pursue current interests and friendships and to experiment with new ones. They are able to accept, as reasonable and fair, the organization and planning which makes such choices possible. They understand that only five can play satisfactorily at the water-table at one time and that the house-corner is overcrowded by more than four. But they cannot exercise their right to choose and to plan their activities if a toddler dithers over whether or not he wants to play with water, because until he 'decides' they cannot know how many places are still available there. Equally, acceptance of that limit in the house-corner breaks down the moment the toddler 'changes his mind' and arrives unheralded in an already full house. His presence offends both those children who have a right to be there and the several children who would have liked to join them if they had known that five occupants were to be permitted today . . .

Apart from the very real difficulties which even the most skilled adults will have in meeting the needs of a group containing both pre-school children and toddlers, and apart from the inappropriateness of such a setting to the toddler himself, I think it is important to realize and to understand the resentment which many of those more mature children will feel towards the hapless toddler.

Any group of pre-school children will contain threes, fours and, if school has not taken them all, fives, at widely differing stages in socialization. Those at the bottom (of the age or maturity range, or both) will be only just ready to learn the social mores and many will still fail to observe them much of the time. These children, themselves under pressure from more mature group-members, will find the unready newcomer intolerable. People who can only *just* manage something are always the ones who are most intolerant of those who cannot manage at all. So, for example, the disgust of this 'just-dry' group when the toddler wets his pants will be extreme.

Children who have fought their way through this stage and learned the social niceties of group-life, will be busy discovering their virtues. The 'bossiness' and 'piety' of many just-fours is a demonstration of this phenomenon. The 'rules' are desperately important to them. They have discovered that 'taking turns' really does mean that each child gets a turn rather than a scrimmage, so they are going to see the queue for that slide observed at almost any cost. When it is spoiled, some will turn furiously on the child who does not understand the point; others will turn away, desperately disappointed to discover that it was not a fair and workable system after all.

At the top end of pre-school maturity, children will have progressed yet another stage. Socialized behaviour will be natural to them now, except when tempers are lost or illness is imminent. It is no effort to them and they may even be capable of understanding that it *is* still an effort for younger children. They may be extremely helpful to newcomers provided those new children show themselves ready to learn. But toddlers who clearly do not care 'how we do things here' will puzzle and then infuriate them. Sad cries of 'but he doesn't take any notice . . .' will resound.

So a mix will work for no one but neither, ironically enough, would provision of separate group-facilities for horizontal age-slices. Those pre-school children do need each other; they do learn skills and tolerance both from those a little more and a little less mature than themselves. The many groups which have been robbed of their four-year-olds by early school entry are thereby impoverished. When a person of three really wants to sing songs, it is good for him to be part of a group containing at least some children who can hold a tune with confidence. And it is good for the older ones to have a period of being 'top dogs' before they become the littlies in a big school.

Those toddlers cannot mix satisfactorily with those bigger children but, by definition, they cannot do so with each other either. An all-toddler group consisting entirely of people from, say, eighteen to thirty months, is a monstrous notion. The children could be kept safe only by total regimentation – which would deprive them of the learning experiences they need – or by the provision of a staff to child ratio which approaches one-to-one. If they are each to have a caring adult for themselves, then group-care becomes meaningless and each toddler could better stay at home with his mother or her chosen substitute.

5. A Different View of Help for Families: Long-term

I am not a politician, an economist or a social philosopher. I cannot hope to lay out a programme for the redirection of society's child-care and I do not propose to make an amateurish attempt to do so. What I do want to do is to set out some of the things I believe each one of us, as individual parents, educators or simply people, could usefully think about, do, or press for, within our own lives and communities.

Attitudes to Babies, Young Children and Their Upbringing

Somehow the idea that bringing up children is a boring, time-consuming and restrictive activity which gets in the way of the important and exciting business of being a female person, has got to change. As I have said, I believe it to be a set of attitudes off the froth of society rather than from its roots. But the froth is what people see and it is not enough for children to *be* important, they have to be seen to be so, too.

New people are a creation, biologically and socially. They are, ultimately, the point of everything else that anybody does and rather particularly the point of those activities which are most generally respected. Without new generations coming along there would be no point in any long-term efforts: no point in painting pictures, devising more equitable laws, developing medical treatments or conserving the countryside. Nobody has to undertake the particular form of creative activity which is

the rearing of children, any more than anybody has to undertake the creative activity of any other profession. But those who
choose to do so should be made aware that they stand with
other creators.

Being somebody's mother is far more than 'just a job'. But
the present social situation puts so much emphasis on the self-
fulfilling aspects of working outside the home that mothering is
actually seen as something less. Yet if one compares low-status
mothering with 'a job' whose high status is generally accepted,
many of the accepted grumbles about child-care fall into a new
perspective. They begin to look silly.

Suppose that you are an architect. You are commissioned to
produce a building which you see as potentially your 'great
work'. Your prideful pleasure in the commission is shared by
everyone around you. Nobody doubts the value of the work
and just embarking upon it brings you high respect. Once you
have embarked upon it neither you, nor anyone else, expects
you to be able to devote much time or energy to anything else
until it is finished. The building will take the lion's share of three
years of your life but, because the end-product is seen as worthwhile, your single-minded devotion is accepted and acceptable.

Architecture is part of the 'real world of work' so,
committing yourself to those years, you do not expect to enjoy
every moment of them. You know that the periods of creative
inspiration will be brief compared with the periods of sheer
hard work. You know that only a little of your time will be
spent doing what only you could do and that the rest will be
spent coping with tiresome, repetitive detail and the tedious
temperaments of your team. You know that there will be
muddy site-visits on wet Monday mornings and endless delays
when your ordered roofing-tiles fail to appear ... You do not
expect it to be non-stop pleasure.

Everyone needs breaks: the architect-you will need them and
so does a mother. Everyone grumbles from time to time about
their working conditions: the architect-you will yearn for a
bigger office or a different firm of builders just as a mother does

for an easier house, a garden or a washing machine. But as an architect you will not moan that it is intolerable of society to expect you to shoulder this responsibility. You wanted it: being given it was an honour. You will not seek a state employee to do some of it for you because sharing it would reduce your status and share of the credit. And you will not seek weapons with which to force your sexual partner to share the job with you. It is yours and he has his. Doing it well is worth every effort you make. The game is worth the candle.

Why is it that we cannot encourage people to feel the same way about their children? Why are we able to accept that a building (or a novel, a sculpture or a garden) is worth the slog when children are not worth the nappy-washing, the broken nights, the repetitive conversations? Why, when we accept elements of boredom or even old-fashioned duty in the working world, are these seen as offensive and retrograde in child-care?

The principal complaint of mothers who want out of child-care is that they are bored. The principal jibe at those mothers is that what they are doing is boring and bound to make them into boring people.

Having enjoyed my own children when they were small as much as I enjoy them now that they are bigger, I am always tempted simply to dismiss such idiocy. I truly find it difficult to understand how anyone can find a developing new member of our race boring *overall* or how facilitating that development could make the facilitator into a bore. Yes; people who are mothering are likely to want to talk about what they spend their days and their thoughts in doing. But that architect yammers on about her job, too, and that is socially acceptable dinner-party talk even among people who have no especial interest in site-subsidence or building regulations.

But if people feel bored it is no use simply telling them not to. When I look at the undoubted advantages which I enjoyed (and still enjoy) in my role as mother, the one which outweighs all the rest – even the decent income, the housing and so forth – is information. It was this, more than anything else, which prevented me from being bored in an all-encompassing and soul-destroying way, even when a particular afternoon or whole week contained no highspots.

The more a mother knows about children's development, about the orderly processes of change, about the actions and reactions which are likely in this or that age-group, in these or those circumstances, the more interesting her own child becomes. The bricklayer who has no way of seeing beyond the wall he has been told to build, cannot share the architect's satisfaction. He is not creating, he is merely working. In the same way a mother who cares for her child without any picture of 'children' and of the potential of her creation, is far more likely to regard the whole business as sheer slog. Interested mothers change mucky nappies, make beds, sweep floors, pick up toys, cook meals and then do it all again, just as uninterested ones do. But they do these external things as a means to an end: to make a comfortable environment for the internal task of relating to the child. They are able to keep their priorities straight: to put themselves and their children before the housekeeping; to keep themselves free of self-imposed domestic slavery.

Women who did not set out to have children because they were *already* interested in them are given little opportunity to get interested after the event. Most people carelessly assume that interest is not necessary because something called 'love' operates instead. Surely love is automatic in a blood-mother? Surely it is this which compensates for anything about mothering which may be at all difficult or tiresome? Of course most mothers do love most of their children; of course it is love which makes much of their mothering possible and enjoyable and of course this is why the parallel with any other creative career is far from complete. But interest and love go together; they support, create and replace each other so that when either one temporarily fails the other takes over and ensures that both mother and child still get what they need.

Interest in the processes of all babies' development makes a mother look and listen carefully to her own baby. It is by looking and listening that she sees the signs of his growing attachment to her and of his individuality. That attachment – his love – reinforces hers and makes her see him as her child because it is to her that he relates. That individuality makes him not just 'a baby' but himself; a unique person who will never be just any human being but will always be himself.

Interest in how babies and children react makes a mother wonder what will happen if she does this, that or the other with her child. That means trying to think herself into his non-existent shoes; and trying to see the world and herself through his senses is part of love. Interest makes her wonder why he cries and what will make him stop. Putting that wondering into experimental action is the same, from his point of view, as loving.

Interest and love do not only support each other on the positive side. They help each other along when everything goes wrong, too. A baby's behaviour suddenly seems unbearable and mothering him an insupportable burden. Love falters, but interest asks why does he carry on like that? Do many children? How do other people cope with it? What will have to happen in this, that or the other area of his development before he is likely to stop? . . .

These vital questions, concerned with the nature and development of children, are not the ones which are answered by the professionals, by the media or even by specialist books on childcare. The information which is poured out to mothers is heavily biased towards the peripheral externals of children's physical lives. Millions of words are expended on subjects like feeding, hygiene or home-safety, yet very few are used to describe this creature who is to be fed, cleaned and protected. No wonder many mothers truly believe that their yucky apricot-rice is more important than their conversation.

The implication is that children are objects to be served rather than people to be loved and enjoyed. The perfect mother therefore uses any time which may be left over from necessary domestic chores in activities designed to make her feel like a television mum and to make advertisers a lot of money. If she has done all the necessary washing, she can buy a special product to get that little sweater 'whiter than white'. If she has made her kitchen clean enough to cook in she can spend a happy afternoon putting special polish on the floor. There seems no limit to the space magazines and newspapers will give to knitting and crochet patterns or to ideas for lining and frilling cribs or making prune-jellies look like baby rabbits. But space for pure interest or for fun? A mass circulation woman's magazine recently asked me to contribute a series of articles on children 'from the psychological point of view'. The editor wanted 300 words per week. She was averaging 2,000 per week on cookery, 3,000 on 'home-making', 1,000 on household gadgets and a four-page pull out on knitting, crocheting or sewing 'for your family'.

In a society which so elaborates the chores of life with a child while ignoring the point of having a child at all, it is no wonder that mothers are predisposed to feeling fed-up. The old image of 'housewife' used to be similar and similarly destructive. We have long ago realized that the business of running a home is peripheral to a couple's happiness and manageable in an enormous variety of ways ranging from ten minutes per day each to dedicated full-time work by one member who happens to like it that way. It is high time that everybody realized that the introduction of a child to that couple *does* demand their presence but does *not* demand domestic slavery. I am typing this sentence while waiting for a batch of jam to jel. But that is because I actually *like making jam*. Doing so does not make me a domestic slave, a domestic bore or a better mother. It just makes me a person who happens to like cooking.

Teaching Child Development

If all mothers, potential and actual, are to be given the chance to become deeply interested in the development of their own children, we are going to have to teach child development to all. It is a dreadfully academic-sounding phrase and this may be partly why people tend to regard it as an academic subject, rightfully the preserve of 'experts'. Maybe we need a new

93

phrase. A national competition to find one would not be a bad start. But linguistics apart, the development of human beings younger than themselves is something which deeply interests almost everyone who is exposed to it. Children, from the age of four or five, love to discuss why they are as they are and not as they were or will be. Schoolchildren are especially fascinated by the group-dynamics which begin to dominate their lives and are often extremely perspicacious about such academic matters as 'scapegoating', 'crowd hysteria' and 'racial prejudice'. As for adolescents, the study of infancy enables them both to look at their own past, as children to their parents, and at their future, as parents of children-to-be. Placed as they are, between age-worlds, they are equally riveted by both. It is sad and silly that we concentrate only on showing them one side of their divide. A few secondary schools – all honour to them – do recognize this. A book of mine is on the syllabus of one local authority and the course has been renamed. Those girls and boys no longer study something called 'mothercraft' which used to centre on a baby doll, but something called 'children'. The course is a popular option. There is even talk of making child development a widely-available option of O-level students. If this is a trend it is better than nothing. But there is danger in formalization. Ought people really to take examinations in 'becoming human'? Like 'sex education' such courses will be only as good as the people who teach them. Diagrammatic representations of the sex act are singularly little help to adolescents trying to cope with first surges of lust. Lists of 'developmental milestones' will feel similarly irrelevant to people trying to cope with one possible result of that lust.

The people who ought to 'teach' child development are the same people who are coping with developing children; they, and only they, are the ones who know how children actually do it. All parents are child-rearing experts in their own right as soon as somebody convinces them that their views, thoughts and actions are of importance. I learned this very early in my professional career when I was sent out, a childless twenty-two-year-old, to administer a questionnaire to parents. I was to ask questions about things like 'peer-group relations' and 'sibling-rivalry' and as long as I got my quota of ticks and crosses, I was doing my job. But I was interested, knew nothing about child-care and felt totally ignorant when face to face with people who were actually *doing* it. I confessed the interest/ignorance and asked for help. I got it. Perhaps those parents did not phrase what they told me in the same way as my textbooks, but they knew what they were doing; they watched their children and thought about what they saw. If I wanted to know, they were keen to tell me. In exchange they wanted to hear from me the views, opinions and methods *other* parents had recounted. This approach gained me a very high interview-acceptance rate. But far more important, it taught me, despite any lingering youthful arrogance, that the real knowledge of child development is right there in children's homes and that a true 'expert' in the subject is only somebody who has listened to and watched as many parents and children as possible and then made patterns of the thousands of individual bits. I have learned almost everything I know from people who are actually doing the job of bringing up children. It is against the scale of actual experience that I measure almost every piece of new academic research.

Using Experts Better

Ours is an expert-ridden society, perhaps an expert-ridden moment in history, and research into child development is accorded the same mystique and unthinking acceptance which is the trend in other fields. I believe that we need to demystify it and, having made it a legitimate topic for everyone's thoughts, to decide what we actually want from experts in it.

The research accumulates massive amounts of information ranging from the particularity of a case study of a single, artistically gifted, autistic child, to the generality of a superficial look at a national sample of seven-year-olds. It all seems very diverse and complex. But, like a computer, which can only produce the answers to questions whose parameters have been programmed in, research can only produce information on topics somebody has already thought of. So child development research does not *create* information about children; it merely examines hypotheses which people have been interested in studying and willing to fund. What they are studying must, by definition, be to do with all of us and our children. The 'infants' of these research workers are, or could be, or might be, our babies.

Part of the mystique lies, as in every field, in the complex, and often totally unhelpful, jargon with which both hypotheses and results are expressed. What pregnant couple is going to realize that a paper entitled 'The ontogenesis of affective relations in the neonate . . .' is about a new baby's first reactions to his caretakers? Part of the mystique lies in the technology research workers employ. If one looks at the instruments set up over that touchingly ordinary carry-cot, it is hard to believe that they are designed to measure something as simple and down-to-earth as the frequency and strength of a baby's sucking. If parents watch a researcher they have invited into their home, it seems incredible that all that video-machinery could really be going to be used to compare this week's kicking with last week's, or that that suitcase full of equipment and forms could be needed to compare their toddler's manual dexterity with that of 'the average' of her age. But a lot of the mystique lies in our willingness, as subjects, to be mystified and as researchers, to mystify. Just as a person who has not bothered to find out how computers work feels that computers might, in some undefined way, 'take over the world', so research workers, especially psychologists, are felt to 'know a lot about us that we don't know ourselves'. It is nonsense, of course.

Research into any aspect of child development and/or child-care begins with children and their caretakers and somehow or other ought to get back to them. Of course research workers cannot be expected to explain every stage of every project to everybody. They would make no progress with the research and the information overload on the mass media would become even worse. But there are ways in which feedback could be ensured if people could be convinced that the information was rightfully theirs and would be useful to them.

One researcher observed the endless trouble which takes place between small wanderers and laggers and their adult companions whenever they are let loose together in open spaces. After watching for a while, he made a careful study of the walking patterns of toddlers and came up with a simple and fascinating discovery: small human beings do not become capable of following, or staying close to, a moving adult until somewhere in their third years. He published his findings in a professional journal and passed on to quite different matters. How many parents ever came to know of his findings? Judging by the cries of 'come *along*, you naughty girl' which seep through my window from the park outside, very few. Yet it is just this kind of information which can serve to interest parents in their children, to reduce the incidence of parental frustration and injustice and to help produce positive handling. If a toddler *cannot* follow, all those old wives' recommendations about 'just keep moving on and he will come in the end' can be clearly seen to lead only to the child being mislaid. A pushchair or a piggyback become obvious and easy solutions.

Magazines published specifically for the parents of young children, as well as the 'under-fives' clubs, sections and columns of women's magazines, spare the space for 'readers' tips' and so forth. Surely they could publish brief 'notes from research' to ensure that parents shared in the knowledge their children's behaviour was giving to the experts? Books on child-care tend to be full of didactic statements for which no evidence is given – ranging from 'babies cry to exercise their lungs' to 'babies never cry for nothing'. Where statements are based on research evidence, I believe that it should be given, just as I believe that where there is no evidence it should be clearly stated that the author is setting out an opinion. Publishers tend to be wary of 'references' in books for the general public. They believe that they make books look 'difficult' and 'indigestible'. But it need not be so. A skilful writer can make the difference between his or her own opinions and established body of knowledge, and the findings of a new piece of research work, perfectly clear. Actual references to the original research papers can be tucked away at the back where they do not bother the casual reader but are nevertheless available to those who want them. Finally, a considerable dissemination of this kind of information can be made simply by researchers having the courtesy to inform their actual subjects of results. It is amazing how often this is neglected. Sometimes it is because the research team wants to keep its true hypotheses from the subjects because if they had known what was really being studied they might have refused to participate. It is common, for example, to study a sensitive area like 'smacking' under the guise of an acceptable generality like 'discipline in the home'. But usually when feedback is withheld it is due to lack of time and resources, coupled with that mystique which keeps people separate from the study of people ... If every individual who agreed to be a subject, or to allow his or her children to be subjects, was told the results in summary, the parental network would do a great deal to spread them by word-of-mouth. In my experience this would also help future researchers to acquire willing subjects.

Few pieces of research are as compact as that study of toddlers' walking. Some are so complex, long-lasting and statistical that it is genuinely difficult to explain them and can be dangerously misleading to try to do so before the work is completed and digested. Continual work is done, for example, on refinements of the 'developmental milestones' which are familiar to most parents. Often this will begin as 'pure research'. Masses of information is accumulated on the ages at which thousands of children learned to sit alone, to crawl or to walk. With those data, an accurate picture of whole populations of young children can be built up. Statisticians then analyse them so that they can be summarized in terms of how many per cent of children did what at which age. Once the work reaches this form, it becomes clearly useful as well as interesting. Those figures can be used, for example, not merely to describe but to compare different groups of children. With further refinements, those same data may be turned into a 'developmental scale' so that the performance of individual children – or of small particular groups – can be measured against those thousands who now constitute some kind of 'norm'. Such a scale, if it works, may then reach the experts who apply research. In their hands the scale may be used clinically, to detect laggards and sprinters; to screen the babies who are seen at well-baby clinics, or to assess the progress of children treated in paediatric departments for a wide variety of conditions. If this kind of work is thrown at the public without extremely careful explanations, it can be counter-productive to all concerned. The information, for example, that 'the average British baby sits alone at 8·3 months' may well alarm the vast numbers of parents whose babies aged ten months are not sitting alone yet. To understand a single statistic (and it is these which tend to be headlined) you need a lot of back-up. What did the sample consist of? What was the definition of 'sitting alone' which was used? What was the age-range which yielded that average figure?

Caution in premature publicizing of this type of work does not mean that the full results should not be made available to anyone to whom they have individual relevance. A mother takes her child to the clinic for his six-months check-up. The doctor who assesses his development tells her that 'He is lagging behind rather badly I'm afraid'. He does not tell her, and she does not feel it is her right to ask, 'Lagging behind what or whom? How do you know?' That original research, which is suddenly of vital relevance to her, does not get past the front-line professional who actually handles her child.

I believe that we often use front-line professionals wrongly and that many of them allow us, even sometimes encourage us, to do so. To me, a professional's prime resource is information *en masse*. While as much information as possible should be open to parents in book form, rather than buried in erudite journals confined to members-only libraries, no parent can hope to read and digest it all. Most parents will only want that part of the existing body of knowledge which is relevant to their lives at any one time. So it is the professional's job to hold the information which constitutes his or her expertise, in trust for parents to use when their personal resources become inadequate. The parent, faced with a problem, goes to the expert to acquire some professional knowledge and information to add to the personal information he or she already has. The meeting should be a sharing; a pooling of resources rather than an instructional, or even a giving, occasion. Each consultation – whether with the local health visitor or the teaching hospital professor – should therefore be educational in the true sense of increasing the parents' resources so that they come away *better equipped to cope for themselves*. A parent who is given reassurance which does not answer secret worries, facts which do not tie up with personal knowledge of the child or instructions which do not mesh with feelings about that child, is reduced and weakened as a parent rather than strengthened by the professional contact.

You call your doctor, on a Sunday evening, to a five-year-old with acute bellyache. Of course the first thing you need is his skilled professional assurance that the pain does not suggest an abdominal emergency. But if he contents himself with saying 'there's nothing the matter with him; just send him to school in the morning, whatever he says,' he actually damages you, as a parent, in many subtle ways. His implied judgement suggests that yours was at fault in calling him. His reassurance does not really reassure because it does not allow for your empathy with your child who is in pain. His instructions seem impossible to follow because they do not mesh with the tenets of good parenting which forbid the banishment to school of children who feel ill.

A good doctor will handle the same situation quite differently. He sees your call as a request for help in coping with a Sunday-night bellyache problem. You have met the problem for the first time; he has met it many times before. He knows that by sharing his extra knowledge with you he can make you better able to cope, not only now and tomorrow morning, but next Sunday night too. So he takes care to acknowledge the reality of the pain just as clearly as he dismisses physical causes for it. He recommends that the child be sent to school in the morning whether the pain continues or not, but he is careful to explain that the child will benefit from discovering that he can in fact manage the new school-week which at present seems unfaceable, and therefore that you may have to be un-characteristically tough in order to help him. He knows that sending the child off will be difficult if he is still complaining, so he suggests some ways in which you can assure *yourself* that you are doing the right thing. He may point out, for example, that the boy may well refuse Monday morning's breakfast but that a good appetite for tea after school will show that all is well. Such a doctor will have given you what you truly sought: the benefit of his advice. He leaves you stronger and more knowl-edgeable as a parent, not demeaned by his expertise.

Unfortunately an abhorrently alienating type of pro-fessionalism seems especially rife in institutions which provide care for children under five. With rare and splendid exceptions, heads of day nurseries, residential nurseries and even nursery schools tend to imply that they know so much about small children in general that nothing about your child in particular can surprise, impress or even interest them. I do not know why this should be so. It may be that being trained to 'manage' the very young *en masse* makes people authoritarian. It may be that having them in groups when they should be in one-to-one relationships makes it impossible to see each as an individual. It may be that the job is so difficult that external behaviours and issues like 'conformity' and 'discipline' become inevitable pre-occupations. It may even be that the family difficulties of most very young children who are in institutional care make the staff feel that they are dealing with failures rather than equals. What-ever the reason, the 'professional image' is positively avoided by many people who want to work warmly *with* parents. The Pre-School Playgroups Association, for example, numbers among its members some of the most highly trained and experienced people in the field. Most of them will not even describe them-selves as 'professional'. As for child-minders, many of those who are currently attending courses in child development keep very quiet about it to the parents of the children they care for.

As one put it to me: 'I wouldn't like them to think I was getting stuck up like that lot over there [the local day nursery]. My mums wouldn't understand that I'm just getting more and more interested the more I do this work . . .'

Training for nursery nurses which will fit them to take a 'casework approach' to parents is being widely canvassed. It shows an awareness of problems in these relationships, but it hardly indicates an approach towards resource-sharing. In the meantime, mothers who insist on trying to share their knowledge of their child with the professional who is going to care for him, risk having the information they give not merely ignored but actually misinterpreted. One such mother made a great point of telling the day nursery matron that her eight-month son never slept in the afternoon and was therefore accustomed to playing on the floor at that time. Later, the matron passed the bewildered baby to a young, trained nursery nurse with these words: 'By the way, don't pick this one up on any account if he cries at afternoon nap-time. He's been thoroughly spoiled and it's up to us to teach him to sleep at the proper times.' Of course the whole message was wrong-headed since you cannot 'teach' a baby to sleep to order; but what was worse was that matron's matter-of-fact planning to re-educate somebody else's baby *without even telling her.* Communication, resource-sharing, was no part of her professional life. The influence of mothers stopped at the door where they put down their responsibility.

Professional educators pay increasing lip-service to involving parents in schools, especially at nursery and infant level. But it is lip-service only. The Association of Head Teachers has just publicly stated that playgroups for three- to five-year-olds are 'no substitute for proper nursery schools run by qualified teachers' (*The Times*, 3 November 1978). Playgroups are run by those un-expert people, parents. Far from truly wanting to involve them in their children's education, the teachers' unions want to push them out. At infant level parent-participation is a meaningless catch-phrase. Apart from appointing a parent or two onto a virtually toothless governing body, it mainly involves telling them, at pre-arranged and ill-attended meetings, what is being done to their children. Parents' self-esteem, and therefore the resources they themselves offer to their children, suffer badly from the clear implication that the school day is 'educational' (valuable) while the the hours spent at home are 'relaxation' (valuable only as preparation for the new school-day or term). Despite the excellence of various reports on the subject – notably that of Plowden *et al*, – few teachers really believe in and act on any kind of genuine partnership between school and home. Their training includes pitifully little material concerned with child development or family life so it is usually only when teachers have children of their own that they become able to see the view from the other side of the school gate. In the meantime most act as if the seven hours per day, five days per week, term-time only, which each of them spends with thirty-something children, were really more influential than the rest of the hours of childhood put together. Crazy? Yes, when it is put like that. But most parents stand back and accept it. Teacher is the expert. She knows best even though they know the child best. Yet it is surely not impossible to think of ways in which teachers and parents could genuinely discuss the children with whom they are all concerned? I once met our son's class teacher in the park on a Sunday. Our casual conversation changed his six-year-old life. We pooled our knowledge of a little boy who did not much like school and, *between us*, we were able to turn him into a child who did. It made both of us feel good, not to mention him. But even she (who I naturally consider an excellent teacher!) left me with the words: 'If only more parents were like you . . .' *They are.* It is the refusal of people like her to consider them in this way which prevents them from showing themselves.

Providing Help Rather Than Escape for Mothers

Because of our attitudes to women's rights and labour and our determined ignorance of the developmental rights of children,

103

the comparatively little money which is spent on provision for the under-fives is almost entirely devoted to various ways of separating them from their mothers. Some theorists (still, fortunately, well-divorced from the practical world) even believe that child-rearing should become an entirely professional activity, mothers being 'freed' from all but pregnancy and labour.

While I accept that there are, and probably always will be, some mothers who truly yearn to escape from the daily care of children they may have been unwise to have, I do not believe that the numbers are nearly as great as the work statistics or the media suggest. I think that many women need only social approval and support to enable them to settle happily to full-time caring for their children. I even believe that some of the women who are currently 'at work', part-time or full-time, are disillusioned with their multiply-complex lives and the concomitant guilty feeling of never doing any of it properly. If they could do so without losing cash and kudos, they too would take their children home.

If there is any truth in this, the most general help which could be given to mothers would be social 'permission' to mother wholeheartedly and clear confirmation to those who are doing so that they have their priorities right. Long-term changes in social attitudes can only be brought about by long-term education, but I do not believe that we have to wait for the long term. A great deal could be done, right now, by taking the wraps off the whole question of young children's need for individual mothering.

Many people do privately believe that babies and small children need this kind of care. Many parents put the belief into practice. But the need is seldom stated, publicly and unequivocally, because spokespeople are afraid of upsetting the parents who do not. I am sorry for mothers who cannot look after their babies themselves, but I do not believe that it is helpful to conceal from them the fact that group-care is a bad alternative. They are entitled to the facts as we understand them and to help in finding *alternatives to themselves* rather than alternative *forms of care*. I am sympathetic, too, with mothers

who could provide full-time care themselves but do not wish to
But they too are entitled to a true picture of the conflict between what they want and what their children need. Only when
they have it can they make informed decisions and, when the
decisions take them away from their children, seek 'good
enough' solutions.

There is a cover-up going on and it is similar to the cover-up
which used to go on over breast-feeding. It has been known for
years that breast-milk was not only the best and safest baby-
food but also an important protection against a variety of
illnesses. But many mothers do not want to breast-feed. In de-
ference to their feelings (and to the social arrangements which
bottle-feeding makes possible) people have walked round and
round those facts, dropping hints and indications but always
building in comforting provisos for the bottle-feeders. With increasingly strong scientific evidence and a change in the climate
of opinion, the wraps are at last coming off. It is now acceptable to state that it would be better if all mothers breast-fed
their babies, at least for a few weeks. As a result, the women
who already take breast-feeding for granted feel good about
doing so; many waverers decide to give it a try and the number
of mothers who are actually unable to produce milk drops dra-
matically. I believe that a similar brave clarity about individual
care would produce similar results.

Since ours is an 'expert-ridden' society, the experts must start
the ball rolling. Books on child-care tend to be packed with
details of babies' physical development and their physical care.
Each and every one of them should also contain information of
the kind I have tried to summarize here, giving parents a clear
picture of what is known of babies' emotional and social development and its relevance to intellectual functioning. The
authors of such books tend to accept that many mothers will
want to work and to quiet their consciences about the probable
effects on babies by making totally unrealistic recommendations to the mothers on coping. One recent and popular book,
for example, does say that if a baby is not to have mother he
will need someone in place of her. But it goes on to suggest

nannies, mother's helps and au pairs. While these may be excellent solutions for the well-to-do, they simply beg the issue for the vast majority of families. Yet by putting them in, by implying that there *are* straightforward solutions available, the author blurs the issue. The reader is left with the impression that leaving the baby is acceptable, so if a mother's help is not available, but a day nursery place is, why not?

Professionally concerned organizations pussyfoot, too, both in consultations with the state and within their own areas. In the reports from which I quoted at the beginning of this book it is clear that they see it as their role to comment on the way child-care *is* rather than the way it could, or, dare I say it, 'ought' to be. Their work is therefore concentrated on suggestions for improving day-care within the context of its existence being taken for granted. None of them dares take the lead in describing that existence as unfortunate and improvement as a matter of phasing it out. I too have worked on working parties. I know how difficult it is to arrive at statements, for public consumption, which all members, representing diverse groups, can agree. But I believe that it has to be done. The National Children's Bureau's official statements are as wishy-washy as all the others. Anything 'controversial' would fail to get agreement. But its chairperson uses her position to speak personally and with courage for the rights of small children to individual care and of the rights of their mothers to give it. How much longer must she remain a solitary individual voice when she is at the heart of government-sponsored research into child development?

One way and another, the government sponsors the training-courses which produce all the professionals who concern themselves with small children, from nursery nurses and nursery teachers to health visitors and social workers. Yet none of these is trained to regard individual care as the ideal against which all solutions to problems in child-care must be measured. At a recent talk I gave to a group of nursery nurse trainees, one girl recounted her worries about the lack of individual attention received by children in her unit. She finished with these words:

'I suppose it's true that they are better off with us. We are taught and we do know what we are doing. But when I have children of my own I shall use everything I know to look after them myself. I'd die rather than put a child of mine in the place where I work . . .' When a mother gets fed up and complains to a health visitor or a social worker, perhaps suggesting that she would like to go back to the outside world of work, nobody tries to see how she could be helped to enjoy herself more where she is. 'Going back to work' is an accepted solution to maternal depression so people offer her lists of day-minders rather than looking at the circumstances which are depressing her. She says that she is 'stuck in all day' and they suggest 'a little job'. They do not ask why she is 'stuck in' and discover that there is nowhere for her to go with her baby. She says that she is lonely and again a job is the obvious answer. They do not ask where her family, her friends, all the neighbours with babies, have got to. If that mother is offered anything at all, it is a way *out of* rather than *through* her unhappiness. A way 'back to work', as if she was not working with her child. A way for her to feel 'useful and productive', as if a new person were not the most useful thing anybody could produce. A way 'to make friends', as if that baby were not panting to give and receive every aspect of companionship and as if there were not dozens of other nearby mothers who were lonely too. Because 'going back to work' is an accepted answer to moments of maternal distress, we offer a route into the guilty, harassed exhaustion of trying to do two jobs at once because doing just one of them was proving difficult. It is as zany as *Alice*; a 'solution' which makes things worse for both mother and child.

The media have a responsibility too. At present, mothers who are getting on with the business of caring for their own children full-time at home, are not interesting. They become so only when something 'unusual' happens – like giving birth to quads – or when they stop doing so to join the trendy world of the 'working mother', or become newsworthy because 'the authorities' take those children away. There is a vicious circle here.

'Just' being a mother is too tedious for media exposure. Because it gets no media exposure it continues to be considered tedious. So it gets no media exposure . . .

If as many viewing hours and column inches were devoted to home-mothering as to mothering-gone-wrong, mothering-avoided and mothering-alternatives, I think a number of important things might happen. The exposure of 'ordinary mothers' to public view would *make* them interesting; to themselves, to the unseen thousands who would identify with them and to the media themselves who, as we have said, first create and then believe their own mythology. Starting the ball of interest rolling would focus parents' attention on what was being done and allow them to see its importance. This would both increase the determination of those who were already giving their children full-time care and would inspire the waverers. As it became clearer to the general public that most mothers do in fact take care of their own children and that they are right to do so, the working-mother image would decline in glamour and come to be seen for what it really is: a necessity for some and a dicey option for others.

If that began to happen, all the various organizations which *are* dedicated to aspects of individualized care for small children, would receive new recognition and begin to be able to pursue their chosen work in an increasingly accepting atmosphere. The Pre-School Playgroups Association, the National Association for the Welfare of Children in Hospital, the National Childbirth Trust's postnatal groups would all fit into a recognized social scheme of things. And because they would lose the faint atmosphere of 'crankiness' with which society taints them, they would gain in membership and strength. That vicious circle could be reversed so that in a few years' time working mothers of small children would feel it necessary to justify themselves for going out, just as full-time mothers now feel it incumbent upon them to prove they are not cabbages.

But 'permission', even social admiration, is clearly not enough help for all mothers. Many women accept the need to stay at home with their small children, but wish they did not have to because they are unhappy, not only with the role but with the way of life. Still more stay at home only because they can find no way, individual or group, of having their children cared for elsewhere. To help them through their child-caring years I believe that we need to bring about a massive redeployment of the financial and professional resources currently devoted to enabling mothers to get out.

6. A Different View of Help for Families: Immediate

Money

I accept that the whole question of paying mothers to stay at home and care for their own small children is a highly controversial one and that public finance is beyond me in its complexity. Nevertheless it seems short-sighted to spend huge sums of public money on poor day-care for children if those same sums – or even smaller ones – could enable mothers to provide good care at home. It also seems downright immoral, in a society which shouts so loudly for equality of opportunity, that rich parents should be able to hire mother-replacements if they wish and middle-income parents be able to afford for mother to stay at home, while only the poor should be pushed out to work by financial need. Of course that is a wild over-simplification because one family's necessities are another's luxuries and the state's view of 'minimum living standards' is always lower than anyone else's. But it is broadly true. A complete family in which the father is on a minimum wage, unemployed or dependent on long-term sickness benefit has a real motive to find the mother a paid job. A single-parent family often has little alternative. Even sparse benefits will not be paid to him or her as of right just because there is a small child to be cared for, hence the priority this group of children is supposed to receive for day nursery places.

As we have seen, a single place in a state day nursery cost £3,800 in capital and £1,130 per year in running costs at 1976 prices. Theoretically parents make means-tested payments but, because of the groups singled out by the priority-system, these are seldom substantial and usually non-existent. At present, the capital costs of state nursery schools and classes are somewhat lower because they do not have to include such elaborate cooking and washing facilities. But their running costs are almost as high because although the ratio of teachers to children is lower than is that of nurses to children, teacher-training is longer and teachers' salaries are higher than those of nursery staff. Furthermore, because they are part of a free education system, parents pay nothing at point-of-service.

If the developments discussed earlier in this book actually take place, educational places for children under-five will inevitably become even more expensive as they will have to cater for children's day-care needs just as day nurseries do now. Placing them in school classrooms vacated by the falling school roll may reduce capital costs somewhat, but professional day-care by the state is clearly going to remain an exceedingly expensive business.

It is possible that an allowance paid to every mother caring full-time at home for her own children under five might actually save public money. The size of the sum payable would no doubt cause hot controversy, but it could reasonably be related either to the individual woman's earnings before childbirth or to the average earnings of the whole work-force. It could be organized much as family allowances are organized now and this would allow the state to claw back in income tax monies which it had inadvertently paid to the rich ... A pipe-dream? Perhaps, but mothers' salaries are already paid, as of right, in several European countries and those of France and Hungary are calculated not on some modest average such as I am suggesting, but on comparability with those of trained infant teachers.

I am not advocating any attempt to work out the true economic value of a mother's job and to pay her accordingly. I have no patience with those who expend hours of calculator time working out a woman's value to her husband in terms of X hours as cook, Y as gardener and Z as call-girl. The things we do with and for each other in the places we call home, are part of being human. We do them for ourselves as well as for others

111

and most men certainly put as much 'unpaid labour' into their households as most women. If the argument is carried *ad absurdum*, we all ought to be paid vast sums of money for deigning to be alive at all. But I am advocating working out the cost to the state of care for those children whose mothers work outside their homes for no other reason than to earn money. And I am advocating distributing that cost to them so that they need not do so.

Of course the economic arguments for encouraging mothers to work are not primarily concerned with how their earnings compare with the costs of state-provided alternative care for their children. The vast majority of working mothers do not use state services but arrange their own, either through family and friends or through private child-minders. They are encouraged by the state because the child-care costs it nothing and the more mothers earn, the more spending money families have to buy things and thus to support production and capital investment in industry. At national level it seems a distorted argument. The effects of the withdrawal of mothers of small children from the labour market would be minimal as their numbers are minute and their hours are short. Furthermore we are in a situation of rising unemployment. While I would never argue that mothers should be *forced* to give up scarce jobs so that unemployed men can have them, I would argue that those who are working reluctantly, and have something else useful to do with their time in the form of mothering, could sensibly be *helped* to free jobs. A mothering allowance, even where it was not balanced by savings in state day-care, would still leave the national budget balanced by the consequent saving in unemployment benefits.

At individual level the argument that going out to work gives a family more to spend is surprisingly often false. As we have seen, the women who are most vociferous about the rightness of all other women working are usually among a tiny, high-earning, high-status minority. If your job brings in £5,000 per year and you have a good accountant, then giving it up is certainly going to make a difference to your living standards and a mother's allowance of, say, £20 per week, is not going to look very tempting. But most working mothers have part-time jobs and both they and their full-time counterparts tend to be employed in low-paid service industries. Going out to work costs a mother money as well as earning it. A privately-arranged day-minder will cost her somewhere between £5 and £10 per week. She has to get the child to the minder and herself to work and back. She may have to lunch in a canteen which, while probably subsidized and excellent food-value, costs her more than she would have spent on bread and cheese at home. She has to shop where she works or wherever she can find time to go, rather than where things are cheapest. She may have to spend more on all manner of personal items – like clothes and hair-dressing – than she would do if she was based at home. And the rush of her life, the conflict of demands upon her, will conceal all sorts of idiosyncratic costs ranging from placatory gifts to minders and children who are upset when she is late, to blower-heaters for speedy warming of a house which has been empty all day and convenience foods for those quick suppers . . . When all these things are taken into account, I seriously doubt whether there are many working mothers with children under five who are contributing a clear £20, or even £15 each week to the net family spending power.

Company and Fun

There is no logical reason why caring for a child or children at home should be a lonely business. I believe that this prime complaint of mothers probably springs mainly from the en-trenched attitudes this whole book has been attacking. We all need to feel approved of, useful, admired when we do our work well and supported when it goes wrong. Depriving mothers of these feelings predisposes them to depression and feelings of worthlessness and futility. But by no means every mother feels like that. I believe that by looking at mothers who are reason-ably content with their lives and talking to them about what would make them positively joyous, we could bring about

changes which would improve lives out of all proportion to
their costs.

One of the principal complaints mothers make is that they are
'stuck at home all day' and that they have 'nobody to talk to but
the baby'. Why? There is nothing in a baby or small child's
needs which demands that he and his mother should stay in one
place all the time, nor, provided he has her presence, is there
anything which demands that she should keep all of her attention
and conversation for him. Almost every mother will be caring
for her child within a community where other mothers are
doing the same thing and, like the parallel 'wanted' and 'for sale'
ads, they will almost all want the company which the others
could offer. So what goes wrong?

Some women are good at making acquaintances – some of
whom turn into friends – simply by getting into casual conversation in the shops or around the parks or wherever they go
with their offspring. The mothers who are happiest in their role
are usually those who have built a network from such acquaintances and are living fuller social lives *with* their young children
than they have ever lived before. But many women find it
difficult to get started, perhaps especially those who live in high
blocks where nobody knows anybody, or in those desolate
streets which are gradually being emptied for demolition, or in
new towns or estates which are designed for a privacy which too
easily becomes isolation.

So the need is for easy, unembarrassing, uncommitting and
inexpensive ways for mothers with babies and young children
to meet each other.

Easy means that whatever 'it' is, it must be right on the door-
step. Some mothers will push a pram, complete with toddler
seat, a mile through the rain to get to somewhere they want to
go, but most will not. The people who are least likely to 'make
the effort' are the very people who most need 'it' – those who
are already over-tired, depressed, fed-up. So it must be close
and it must be casual. No forms to fill in, no dressing-up re-
quired.

Unembarrassing and uncommitting go together. They mean

all kinds of different things to different people, but most mothers would agree that there must be no implication that they are seeking help, in trouble, looking for guidance. There must be no nosey-parkering by 'them' and no prior necessity to register, commit yourself for the future, or hand out your name and address. The privacy which easily becomes isolation remains precious. Few mothers want to feel that if they emerge once, somebody will be ringing their doorbell if they choose to stay at home tomorrow.

Inexpensive is not so simple as it sounds. Free is cheap, but if what is received for free comes from 'the authorities' it has to be carefully presented if it is not to fall into the 'embarrassing' category. Most mothers accept free premises, heat, light and so forth without thinking about them. We are all accustomed to libraries and parks. We do not pay admission and we know, if we think about it, that we do, in fact, pay for them all through our rates. But those proverbial cups of tea are usually far more acceptable on the basis of cheap-because-bulk-ordered than actually *free*. You cannot 'stand yourself one' or buy one for a friend if it does not cost anything.

So what should 'it' be? Many different schemes have been, and are being, tried in various parts of the country ranging from highly-structured groups with a purpose – such as those run by certain voluntary organizations for parents and their handicapped children – to entirely self-instigated groups consisting of mothers who discover that they all live in the same village. There is probably a place for all and more of them. But nobody can start, or pay for, something that is so variegated as to be invisible so, since I want people to start and pay for 'it', I must choose a something to describe.

The best model I know is the council-run one o'clock club. These usually consist of a play-hut (with or without lavatories and kitchen) together with outdoor playspace and one or two paid staff. They are 'clubs' in name only. They have no membership, no structure, they simply exist. Within them mothers can, and do, make whatever they want and need. And it is the variousness of the results, reflecting the variety of the needs, which makes me single them out as models; starting-points for possible further development.

I know two such 'clubs' intimately. The first operates entirely casually. It is there. The hut is warm and dry and has a lot of rather shabby toys together with such hard-to-provide facilities as sand and water and a climbing frame. The outdoor space is safely fenced from the park in which it stands. There are trikes and dolls' prams, a swinging rope and, by happy chance, a sandy hillock. Mothers drop in with their children either because it is wet and the children can play there without causing a chaos of clearing up at home, or because it is fine and therefore a good day for the park. They chat to any other mothers who may be there; play with their children or watch them squabble with each other, and then they drift away again. Of course friendships are sometimes made there. Of course people sometimes arrange to go with friends. But the place has no club atmosphere; no mutual support function. Its regulars – and there are a lot of them – do not want it to have. They just want it to be there when they feel like using it. But the fuss, the misery, when for six weeks it had to be closed for repair . . .!

The second 'club' is almost identically appointed but it has been turned by its regular users into a complete resource-centre for parents and their under-fives. It is a daily playgroup without registration; an advice centre without experts; a swop centre for everything from prams to skills. Now it is becoming an emergency centre too. A babysitting and mother-substitution scheme is just getting under way stimulated by the illness of a regular mother who could not bear the thought of her children being sent to strangers while she was in hospital.

At present these clubs are rate-supported and therefore free to the consumer. Their staff are council employees, mostly mothers with their own under-fives, who welcome a part-time job where their motherhood and their children are both integral. They are extremely cheap to run and could, I believe, be even cheaper. Somebody does need to be on the premises from the time when the doors open to the time when they close.

Without this, mothers will sometimes arrive to find nobody and they will sometimes arrive to find a mess and a muddle because yesterday was a day when nobody felt like clearing up. But I do not believe that such people need to be trained playleaders or indeed trained anything, provided they will be pleasantly welcoming to all-comers and reassuring to those who, peeping in for the first time, find it difficult to believe that they need nobody's permission or authority to use the place. In most areas I believe that this could be done by a rota of mothers, each perhaps paired with a stand-in lest somebody comes down with mumps. Toys and equipment are needed to start off with, but once launched they could be almost self-sustaining. One family's cast-off toys are novelties to another; the things that now go to the jumble sales can go to the club and there is always somebody who is good at getting invaluable junk from the local shops or factories. A small block-grant, for the purchase of paint, plasticine, scissors and so forth, combined with enthusiasm from a mixed group of mothers *and* fathers would deal with the whole matter. If every council would provide a prefab in the corner of every park or gardens, count its structural maintenance in with the budget of the parks department, check it for fire and hygiene regulations, but otherwise let it alone, it seems clear that each club would become whatever its users wanted of it. And if there is no park or gardens? Shame on us and we shall have to site it in the grounds of the estate or on the corner building-site that has been a junk-dump for five years ... Tea? If the people who go there want to think how to provide it. Health visitor? If they invite her. Safety regulations? But these children are with their own mothers ...

The whole point of these 'neighbourhood clubs', as they might be called, is that nobody should impose upon the mothers and children who use them any kind of structure or any pre-conceived notions about how they should be used. But I believe we need more structured groups as well. If a mother is already lonely, depressed, out of her culture or simply painfully shy, she may not have the personal resources either to use an unstructured situation or to take part in structuring it. She needs to become replenished as a whole, autonomous, self-determining person, before she can enjoy being expected to behave like one.

In many ways the Pre-School Playgroups Association playgroups fulfil this more structured role for mothers with children between three and school age. The 'new' mother finds herself offered a play-learning environment for her child in which she can involve herself as much or as little as she feels able. The playgroup is there and open at its stated hours. The responsibility for its minute to minute activities is not hers. She can sit and watch if she wishes; she can even leave if her child is settled; but she is continually invited, overtly and covertly, to involve herself in what is going on and, above all, to understand and to share the experiences her child is having. With most of the attention focused on the children and their activities, she need not feel that the eyes of the old hands are on her. She can find a place gradually at her own pace and eventually, almost always, she will make her own contribution to the group as a whole and know that she is valued and valuable. For mothers with pre-school children we need more and more such groups and we need ways of keeping them economically viable without pricing them into the exclusively middle-class market to which many people wrongly believe them to belong. Playgroups need more state money but not more state interference and getting the one without the other will be difficult. The 'by parents, for parents and their children' philosophy, which keeps them as generators rather than replacers of parental resources, is already threatened by ideas about 'integrating them into other services for children under five'. The idea of running *this* kind of playgroup 'under the supervision of' an attached day nursery or child health clinic, is anathema. To be an extension of parental resources, playgroups have to belong to, to be run by and be the responsibility of, the parents of the children who use them. The anxiety of the state to ensure that children are kept safe and are 'properly' cared for is commendable and their fear of liability in case of accident is understandable. Nevertheless if playgroups are to function as parent-resources the state will have to trust them to know best. If they do not, playgroups will become more and more like nursery schools; places which parents accept as being of benefit to their children but from which they, personally, tend to flee.

By the time children reach an appropriate age for playgroup, their mothers are through the most isolating years of caring for them. The need for semi-structured groups for those with babies and toddlers is even greater and for this there is as yet no entirely satisfactory model. Mother-and-baby and mother-and-toddler clubs spring up all over the country but they die down again with equal rapidity. Many operate only once each week and while a weekly treat can be far better than nothing, it is not nearly enough to alter life if the walls of home are closing in on you. Some groups suffer from lack of organization because the mothers who are trying to keep them going are continually disorganized by their small children's unpredictable nap-times or recurrent colds. Some suffer from over-organization, with two or three mothers determinedly shouldering the responsibility and unwittingly becoming an in-group which leaves potential members feeling embarrassed to join in. But perhaps most of the groups which die out do so because their initial impetus drains away, or leaves the district, and there is no obvious 'point' to keep the group in being.

While these groups are primarily needed to provide a companionable network for mothers, I think they will probably always function best when they have an additional and external purpose. The idea of a 'purely social' club is as embarrassing to many mothers as it is to lonely people in other stages of their lives. A look at some of the clubs which are currently successful tends to support this view. Many pre-school playgroups now have a mother-and-toddler club run in conjunction with them. The mothers see them as stepping stones towards the playgroup-proper and they share not only the premises and equipment but also the experience and the ethos of playgroup people. In an ideal world there would be more playgroups and every one would have a separate room for mothers and younger children ... Some voluntary organizations arrange groups for parents whose children are handicapped. The purpose of providing special help for special children leads mothers to make tremendous efforts to use and to keep in being anything which is started for their benefit. In the United States clubs flourish for twins and their mothers and a study of British twins, in which I took part some years ago, suggested that mothers of twins here, too, would welcome close contact with each other. I believe that less traumatic and unusual factors in their lives could also be used to help mothers to feel linked together in some common purpose and able, even bound, to support each other through the early years of child-care.

Locality is vital. Sometimes simply living in the same community is enough to give mothers the purpose of improving that community for themselves and their children. Something that begins as a pressure group to keep that playground open may turn into something that stays in existence to keep everybody sane. Sometimes a few mothers who happen to find themselves in contact will stay together as a babysitting group or a swopping group or a bulk-buying combine. In my own district, an American mother owned a cold-air vaporizer and was encouraged, by the local general practitioner, to lend it to those of us whose children suffered from croup. That gadget, then unknown in British homes, led to a network of local friendships and to the eventual lending of all kinds of things which none of us needed often but which we all needed badly when we needed them at all. Our camping cot went the rounds and three Baby Alarms served about twelve families . . . One family always has, or has access to, more than enough of things that other families cannot get. Once they have met each other it seems obvious that one father's excess of used computer-paper for painting on should go to as many children as possible, while his own children should be able to benefit from the next family's surplus of rabbits, blackberries or sheer, glorious space. Does it all sound terribly cosy? Well, it can be cosy and when it is there need be nothing terrible about it. If people are parents, trying to make the best possible life for themselves and their children, amid other people who are doing the same, all will be enriched by every sort of interchange.

But before local causes and conveniences can serve as a linking purpose between families, they have to know that each other is there. Since almost every mother-to-be attends antenatal classes which are locally organized and has her baby in a hospital with a local catchment area, pregnancy seems the obvious time to bring this awareness about. The National Childbirth Trust already encourages local groups of mothers to continue the mutual support function, engendered during preparation for childbirth, after it is over. Many of its groups are working well and there is no reason why similar encouragement should not be given to women attending 'ordinary' antenatal classes. A 'fathers' evening', for example, is usual towards the end of the course. Make it a little more social; encourage people to *talk* to each other rather than merely listening to an expert lecturing, and some, at least, will discover that they are close neighbours with babies due in the same week ... Once a woman is in labour she is unlikely to care whether or not any of the women around her come from that class. But once she has her baby, why can she not be asked whether or not there is anyone else in the ward whom she already knows? If maternity-ward staff were conscious of serving a local community and conscious of the importance of that community to the women they serve, they could do much to foster such friendships. When a new mother takes her baby home, she may well be emotionally submerged so that she cannot make the effort of contacting those whom she met when she was pregnant. But those six-week check-ups could be organized on a local basis so that acquainted mothers met up again. The health visitor, making her statutory visit to each newborn, could carry news from one to another; and well-baby clinic staff could offer routine appointments in batches based on shared antenatal course attendance.

Of course not every mother will want this kind of 'putting in touch' but the ones who do not will tend to be the ones who do not need it because they already have a friendship or family network which is sufficient for their needs. Of course being put in touch will not work for everyone because just having a baby does not necessarily make you the friend of everyone else nearby who has one too. But it does predispose you that way, and at least if you know who is around you have a choice between company and aloneness. And, to a large extent, choice itself banishes loneliness.

But I do not believe that the possibilities are limited to contacts made at birth or soon after, or through the professionals every mother has to stay in touch with. I believe that the need for easy, uncommitting, unembarrassing and inexpensive contacts and company can be met within the commercial world, too. Ironically this idea shocks many people. We have got it into our heads that mothers and small children are either nothing to do with us or need 'service'; that service should be free and benevolently authoritarian, run by 'them' for 'us' (or the other way around, depending where you are standing just now). To justify its existence it should at least smack of do-goodery. While there is certainly a place for this kind of 'service' – and I am coming to it shortly – I do not believe that service facilities are necessarily the kind which mothers need to make their lives fuller of enjoyable company. Where does a single adult go when he or she wants to be with other people, feel part of the social world, yet not make the effort of 'joining' something? What about a coffee bar or café? I believe that if the existence of mothers and small children in the community were sufficiently recognized for entrepreneurs to look into it, they would find that one of these could be set up with them in mind in every shopping centre, large and small, throughout the country. It would need space for a play-area and this would put the rental up, but everything else that it would especially need – from toys and play-equipment to special floor-coverings and safety heaters – would be forthcoming free from manufacturers. They would not be slow to realize that a user-shop-window is the best kind of advertising of all. During the past three years I have watched this aspect of the idea working at four separate toy exhibitions – two in London and two in country towns. Each was open for several weeks and each provided a large range of toys and equipment both for children to use on the spot and for parents to buy if they wished. Many of the vast numbers of mothers who attended would have endorsed the words of one: 'Having this here has been like having fairyland for the kids and a club for me right smack in the middle of town. We've been most days this week 'cause it's closing soon, more's the pity. Yes, I have bought a few odds and ends, but they don't make you, you know. They know they'll make their money back at Christmas ... Anyway what does it cost them really, putting their samples here for the kids to use? I mean we know it's for the advertising but oh! we shall miss it when it goes ...'

Right-thinking manufacturers would not have to confine themselves to advertising and sales either. What better place could there be to do research on new products? Companies pay endless amounts of money to market researchers to test the sturdiness of that toy or the desirability, to small children, of this particular colour ... Let them come and watch; let them talk to any coffee-drinking mothers who are prepared to talk to them. Let them see for themselves whether the orange juice stains that floor covering.

I think that this idea would work particularly well for the very mothers who are least likely to make much use of 'neighbourhood clubs' or 'mother-and-baby groups' and who find it most difficult to stay in touch with friends made in pregnancy or to follow up on contacts arranged for them by the child-care specialists. Coffee bars and shops do not make you feel obligated; they require neither your best behaviour nor your gratitude. They do not even remind you of an authority from whom you may already feel alienated. Every university district has one or two coffee bars which have been unofficially adopted as student meeting-places just because they are in the obvious place. Most big factories, railway yards and other work-places have the same. Mothers would go to these in the same way; just because they were the obvious place to go, and fun for their children. And because they *were* the obvious places to go mothers would automatically come into contact with others who were doing the same thing. Toddlers and older children would compel friendships, even among the shyest, because every mother eventually becomes not only Mary Jones, but also Johnny's mum.

The basic idea has all kinds of ramifications. Big stores would get far more custom from mothers if they provided such a place instead of the usual snack bar which has no space and disapproves of kids. By using drink and snack machines to replace most of the human staff, places where mothers already have to go, like launderettes and libraries, could provide the same. It would be an obvious combination with a toy shop. It might even lead to the kind of secondhand and swop shop I have always dreamed of. The place where you buy the endless equipment every child needs and to which you return it when he has grown out of it and needs something else.

What about a very large commercial rate-rebate for anyone who wants to try it out? What about rent-free use of premises which are already empty, a privilege already given to many charities?

Working Conditions and Fun

If you look around a suburban street in the daytime, a very large proportion of the people you see will be mothers with children below school age. Yet look at that street again and you will see that almost nothing about it takes cognisance of them. It is as if no town planner, councillor or architect ever had a young family. Or as if, and this may be closer to the truth, no mother ever reached seniority in such a profession. Over the past few years there has been increasing pressure on such people to make provision for the needs of physically-handicapped people within the community. Yet few of them seem to realize that life is almost as difficult for a mother with a pram or pushchair as it is for an adult in a wheelchair. In my ideal society a Children's Community Rights Act would be regarded as at least as essential as a Sex Discrimination or a Race Relations Act. And if that sounds like a joke, I wish it did not.

But, as every social reformer knows, legislation is only effective to the extent that it is socially accepted. We could ban, by law, some of the most glaring injustices to mothers and small children; we could insist, by law, on the provision of some facilities for them. But what is really needed is a general recognition of their existence and of their worth. They spend their nights and their days between their homes and their local districts. So their home conditions are their work conditions; they have no carefully-inspected factory, regulated as to light and heat, safety and comfort, to escape to. Their productivity is what they do together; and they have no employer anxious to get the best from them nor union to swop work for reward. If anybody cared, there are innumerable things which could be done to make their lives easier and to make them more fun. Many of them would cost nothing. The money spent on some of them could be recouped from the mothers themselves, while some of the most expensive measures would repay their cost through savings to the emergency services in accidents and family breakdown ... Most of what I am going to suggest will sound – to everyone but a current parent – like trivia. Each issue is, by itself, trivial. But daily life with a small child is made up of endless successive minutes of trivia and each pin-prick adds to the next to make the soreness of being 'stuck at home' and 'bored out of my mind'.

The mother who does not want to be stuck in the house all day has to go out. To do so she has a few little problems nobody can remove like getting coats on to small reluctant bodies as well as her own, but having accomplished those she may have to go downstairs in a lift. It is designed to let adults in and out and it has no special gadget to hold the door open while she manoeuvres herself, a pram and a toddler safely inside.

If the lift is broken she, like other residents, will have to walk down. But unlike other residents she may be totally stuck. She cannot push the pram downstairs. Even if it folds and she can carry it, she cannot carry pram and occupant together nor leave

125

a baby on the ground alone at either the top or the bottom ...
If she has a toddler as well as a baby she can neither carry both
of them together nor leave either one alone at either end. Not a
very good start.

Perhaps the lift was not meant for prams. Perhaps she is even
provided with a pram-store at the bottom? Fine, but babies use
their prams as portable beds in, as well as out of, the house, so if
that is the case she needs two. Does anybody who puts a young
family to live in an upstairs flat give her a 'necessary second
pram' grant?

Once down and out, she is in a street. Wherever she is going
she will eventually have to cross it. The traffic scene is beyond
the scope of this book, but even within the present ghastly situation in which roads belong to cars rather than to people and
those who drive them forget the times when they take the role
of pedestrian, there are some measures which could ease her
way. Kerbs are hell both for pram-pushers and for pram-riders.
We urgently need more smoothed-out places where they can be
avoided. At present kerbs stand proud of the road and flush
with the pavement, the idea being that they keep cars from
joining the walkers. But many road accidents to very small children take place because walkers join the cars. Why cannot kerbs
stand proud of pavements, too? A four-inch rise would prevent
that fatal dash into the traffic because the child who tried it
would fall over instead. The new kerbs would make pram-life
worse, but with more sloped crossings that would not matter.
As a corollary to the new kerbs there should be a new, automatic and highly expensive traffic offence: that of driving any
vehicle, under any circumstances, on to the pavement. At present putting your nearside wheels on to the pavement is an
accepted method of getting your car – or delivering lorry – out
of the traffic flow. Nobody seems to realize that wheels on the
pavement make nonsense of everything parents try to teach
young children about the pavement being safe and the road not
being so. Of course if the mother we are accompanying happens
to live in the country she may find herself on a road which has
blind corners, large farm vehicles, drivers who assume that

there is no oncoming traffic *and no pavement at all.* Just where is she supposed to walk safely with that pram?

Prams and pushchairs are designed to push rather than pull so when she needs to cross the road the mother must shove her baby into a river of motorized metal in order to demonstrate her intention to drivers. Let us hope there is a pedestrian crossing for her and that all the cars, even the ones in the far lane, really stop. In the middle of the road there will probably be a refuge but it will not be big enough to take the whole pram. It should be big enough for that and it should be partially railed, too. Without rails how is she to keep her toddler safe while watching for the right moment to cross the second half of the road?

Panda crossings and their relations are a disaster and should be rethought. The time allowed for pedestrians is only just enough for the hale and hearty adult. If her toddler falls down the mother will be in trouble. When did you last hoot at a tiresome group which held you up after your light went green?

In a very busy area the mother may find an under- or an overpass. But with a pram, she will not be able to use it. Without slopes instead of, or as well as, steps, these crossings cannot be used by many of the people who need them most.

Perhaps that mother would like to use public transport? Well, with a pram she will just have to want. Even a folding pram cannot be closed up with one hand while holding the baby with the other, even if the toddler will stay safely close by while you try. You cannot put a baby down on the pavement while you fold the pram, so it is hopeless. With a pushchair she can have a try. Not the tube, though. Folded pushchair in one hand, toddler in the other, on an escalator? No, thank you. A bus perhaps? Well, yes, if there is a conductor to help her on and somewhere to stow that pushchair once she gets aboard. Yes, again, if the downstairs seats were kept for her as well as for non-smokers and if the driver had been taught to glance over his shoulder to make sure she was seated before he let his clutch in ... I wonder whether it ever occurs to the people who park their cars on bus stops to wonder how mothers with young children will enjoy getting out into the middle of the road?

127

Probably she does not need public transport but is only going to the shops. Fine, but will the shops let her take the pram in with her? Probably not. She cannot leave it outside with the baby in it or he may get snatched, jostled or teased so at present she will have to take him out and risk the empty pram getting stolen. Most shops could provide space for prams near the checkout counters, but they would have to get rid of their swing or revolving doors. A good thing too as both are murder when you are carrying a baby or have a small child at foot. You can get hurt or separated or both. Shopping is not much fun with a baby to carry and even less so if you have a toddler to steer as well. People only have two hands, you see. In supermarkets the toddler seats on the trolleys help a bit but their age-range is very limited. There is a nice design-project here for a student. In the meanwhile why are mothers not allowed to use their prams or pushchairs instead of trolleys? How difficult would it be to provide them with carriers belonging to the shop so that the purchases could be counted out of them at the end?

'All shoplifters will be prosecuted' says the notice, but there, at the checkout counter, just where the toddler must wait in an incomprehensible queue, are the bars and bars of chocolate, piled into bins just his height. He did not shoplift that Mars Bar he is eating, paper and all, did he? She was always going to pay for it, truly she was. People with not much shopping do not see why they should queue for long so they have special express checkouts. But why should those children have to wait? Where are the special checkouts for them and their mothers? Rich ladies who can tip, get their shopping carried out to their cars. But where is the packer who will help a harassed mother get her impossible load organized? How difficult would it really be to provide a few highchairs with safety harnesses so that she could park the baby while she found her money or went back for what she had forgotten?

Where next? The library perhaps. But there are steps up to the door (pram trouble again) and anyway the adult librarian will glare and say 'Ssh'. The Children's Library probably does not open until after the schools let out and it may well have a minimum lending age of five. Many such librarians take their work extremely seriously and do a marvellous job in helping school-age children with books for projects and hobbies as well as for pleasure reading. But dismally few provide the hours, the sincere smiles and the mats on the floor which would enable our mother to spend a happy hour there with her children. Anyway that toddler will certainly not be allowed to touch any books today because his hands are showing that Mars Bar. She would have to wash him first and where can she do that?

Every mother who gets out and about with small children needs public lavatories. Babies soil themselves and when they do, they stink, which is unpleasant for all. The only answer is to change their nappies and you cannot do that in the street. Toddlers who are 'dry' usually feel very strongly about staying that way but cannot do so for nearly as long as adults. Boys can pee down a drain if their mothers are French or brave. Girls are more of a problem and anyway it is not always a pee that is needed. So we need more, many, *many* more public lavatories. But even when there is one, in the right place and at the right time, the parents' troubles are not over. A father with a small girl must choose between taking her past that uncompromising row of backs at the Men's urinal or sending her alone into the Women's. A mother with a small boy must either offend his dignity by lifting him up to *sit* on an adult lavatory or send him alone into the Men's. Perhaps we shall soon have unisex facilities as in most of Europe. Certainly every public lavatory should have a child-sized loo in a cubicle whose lock can be undone from outside with a coin when the child gets stuck. All our 'Ladies' already contain slot-machines for sanitary towels so why on earth not add machines to dispense disposable nappies and paper pants for the days when it gets left too late? We have mirrors and dressing-tables as well as washbasins, so why not a changing counter as well? Nobody has thought about it, that is why.

The baby is getting fed up now. She did not have a Mars Bar. But is there anywhere for the mother to feed her? Perhaps there is a bench or seat but if there is it will probably be placed directly on the kerb, inside a row of parked cars. If she sits there with the baby how is she to keep the toddler out of the road? I wonder what it would cost to put arms and a bar across one end of every street-side or park bench so that anyone old enough to sit at all could safely be sat there for a few minutes? A decently aware society would go further. We provide shelters for people waiting for buses, so why not shelters or refuges, pavement bays if you like, where mothers could get out of the stream of people for a few minutes, sit down, wipe mouths, readjust loads, or just restore screaming muscles and tempers?

If the baby is breast-fed such a public place is no good. With our negative attitude to babies and their needs the mother will be stared at, glared at and whistled out of countenance. She might even get 'spoken to' by a policeman. It is not actually illegal to breast-feed a baby in public but 'disturbing the peace' covers anything the law-enforcer pleases even if a suckling baby is one of the most peaceful sights you are ever likely to see. Armed with a bottle, she can retire into a café if there is one. But the toddler cannot reach the table from the only available chairs and there is no room for both children on her lap. He wants orange squash and it comes in a sealed carton into which you push a straw. He has not yet learned to drink through a straw and taking off the lid so that he can use the container as a beaker sounds a great deal easier than it is, especially one-handed. The mother could have a cup of tea. Indeed if she is going to occupy the table she will have to have something. But the baby's hands are waving perilously close to the hot liquid and there is nowhere she can be put down while mother drinks it. Even without my mothers' coffee bars it seems extraordinary that ordinary local cafés do not cater for small children and their mothers. All they need are high chairs and/or baby seats; beakers with handles; half-portions on request; dampened tissues for mopping up and the kind of tolerance which agrees to provide a buttered roll *without* the standard ham . . .

Probably it is time to make for home now, but as a walk with some fun in it. After all this is meant to be an outing. Look around and see what there is for mother and toddler to see and do together. There are many adults and some of them are pursuing fascinating jobs which he would love to watch. But most of them are hidden from him. The cobbler is tucked away at the back of his shop, the counter of the dry-cleaners is too high for him to look over at the steam-presses and the scales of the greengrocer are too high for him to see how many potatoes make five pounds. Children are *small*. Railed library steps are ideal, but even a box to stand on makes the ordinary everyday environment more usable.

There are lamp-posts all down the street and in some areas there will be flower baskets on them. Lovely; the toddler can try the colours of those geraniums and he might even see the man from the council on one of those lorry-platforms they use for watering them. There could be bird-feeders on them, too . . .

There is a building-site on the corner with all kinds of fascinating machines. But high hoardings ensure that the toddler cannot watch. A few holes, two feet six inches from the ground and he would be able to see it all.

They walk along beside the railway and then over a footbridge. Of course that line has to be safely fenced-off but why must the fence be solid? Do people not know that children like to watch trains? On the bridge his mother lifts him perilously up to watch a train pass beneath them. Later he will climb, even more perilously, to watch. If peep-holes had been built into the concrete he could have watched in safety. In a society which realized that some of its members were small, every barrier which adults look over would have peep-holes for looking through.

Doing is even more important than looking when you are small. The toddler has mother's letters clutched in his hand and he recognizes the friendly red postbox. But of course he cannot post those letters because he cannot reach. The postmaster tells me that special low slots would be 'inadvisable' because 'children would post rubbish'. Who is it that posts fireworks and french letters? Not people three-foot high but the five-feet people who should know better.

After the postbox they come to a remote-controlled crossing.

131

It will be years before the toddler is safe out alone in 'his' community, but his mother would like him to see the connection, again and again, between pushing the button and that little green walking man coming on. But he cannot reach to push it. He cannot reach *any* of the buttons which control his difficult, automated environment, not the ones at crossings or on buses nor the ones which summon lifts or ask people to let him in through front doors. So he cannot start to learn until he is much bigger. But think what could be done with this pleasure in posting and pushing things if anyone actually wanted that toddler to have fun. Rubbish bins could have posting slots and he would pick up sweet papers for the fun of posting them. Buttons to push could control a glory of tiny joys all along the street, like little mirrors whose covers slide back so that you can see yourself, or chimes that ring when you press. No, these are not meant to be *useful*, they are meant to be fun.

What else can they do on the way home? The corner-shop is a favourite place and the shopkeeper is a familiar dispenser of goodies and therefore a good person to practise talking to. There ought to be an especially low section of counter for those conversations to take place across, but of course there will not be. Having a corner-shop at all is luck these days. A few know all the local families by name, keep special pocket-money lines for children and care enough to keep the rules about who may buy cigarettes or fireworks. They serve as a vital link in the community chain with an importance far greater than their turnover would suggest. Yet one by one they are rated out of competition with the big chain-stores and vanish, leaving their districts impoverished. If the local pub were forced to close by economic pressure from the road-house a mile away, the uproar would fill the local paper. But the corner-shops are only important to the old and to mothers and children. Nobody makes much fuss.

They will almost certainly pass a launderette and doing some washing there can be quite fun. But given that almost every family will use it and that a high proportion of the clothes washed there will belong to children, is it not extraordinary how little notice is taken of them? Once again, they cannot reach the slots and the buttons. There are chairs and magazines for adults but nowhere for children to sit and nothing for them to do. Is it lack of money or imagination which prevents the owners (who are in it for money, after all) putting in a few child-size washing baskets, a washtub for dolls' clothes, a toy iron or two ... These are the customers of the future, Sir, and what is more their mothers will come to you, rather than to your competitors, if you show them that you know what doing the family wash with most of the family under your feet can be like.

Perhaps there is a 'gardens'. If there is nothing, no patch of grass anywhere on which the family can pause, sit, play, look, then it is because nobody has thought or bothered. Most streets could provide a patch at least the size of an ordinary back-garden; even that is enough to make an oasis in the child's concrete world. Unfortunately most of our odd corners are devoted not to the grass children need, or to the cafés they would hold almost anywhere else in Europe, but to the motorcar.

If there is a gardens it may well be a pretty place to move *through* rather than a place *to be*. Neat tarmac paths will run through green and shrubbery which is somebody's pride and joy and firmly marked 'Keep off the grass'. The keeper will not yell at the lonely dogs who break his rules; after all they have to go somewhere, don't they? But let the mother spread a rug for that baby and produce a ball for the toddler and he will move them on. It is for looking at, not for using. The toddler may see, but he may not do. If he tries to feed the pigeons from his mother's newly-bought loaf, he will be told that he is messing up the paths. Pigeons can do damage in towns, so why are there no half-coconuts hanging in the trees to attract the smaller birds first to their flesh and then to bathe in their rainwater? Why is there no dispenser, complete with reachable money-slot and buttons, from which he can purchase nuts or seeds to feed to them?

If he climbs on the seats he will be scolded for putting his feet where elderly ladies want to put other portions of their anatomy. But climb he will, so why not put something for him to

133

climb? Those sharp metal railings could be cheap and friendly wooden post-and-rail and he could climb those to his heart's content. Year after year councils spend money on removing branches pruned from city trees. Pile them here and he could climb over, jump off and straddle them as they turn from horse to motorbike. Let them collect insects under their rotting bark; insects are part of his world and he needs an introduction. Let them gather moss for him to stroke.

Acorns and oak-apples fall each autumn and are quickly whisked away, with the dead leaves, as rubbish. But why? Leave the fruits and they will attract the squirrels and the bigger birds which could make this little urban gardens into a magic place for small children. Competing with them, children can make collections, grow the seedlings in jam jars, and find the leaves which have turned to skeletons. And those leaves: we are rearing a generation of children many of whom will never have spent an October afternoon jumping in a leaf-drift. To me, that is almost as sad as believing that Cheddar cheese is mined from the Gorge as suggested on television.

Why is it all kept so neat, tidy, unused and sterile? Who is it for, if it is not for mothers and children? If you actually ask them, keepers either say that the gardens must be tidy for 'the old folk' or for the supervisor. But we pay that supervisor to use the land to fill our community's needs and mothers and children are needful members of the community. As for the retired people who may, or may not, sit there and contemplate the past what makes us think that they want the gardens tidy and empty? Is this not the kind of place where young and old could meet and share?

So the mother and her young children make their way home. No disasters have struck. The mother did not drop her purse down a grating, up-end the pram with her shopping, lose the toddler . . . But it has been an effort rather than a pleasure and all three of them have got less out of the trip than they could have done. If we turn away from the realism of the kind of thing mothers do almost every afternoon, and look instead at the possible 'treats' in their lives, the opportunities which we miss on their behalf become even clearer.

Begin with parks. Britain is rich in them and London is world-famous for its breathing-holes. They are obvious places to take small children. A park offers wide open spaces and infinite potential for new experience, for excitement, for adventure – or does it?

'Our' park caters well for many other age-groups. Their football pitches and running-tracks dominate the scene and take up all the parkland that is close to the entrances. To escape organized sport, laden mothers must walk on. All the grass is mown, and to facilitate the machines, the land is kept as flat as possible. Lumps and bumps on which a small person could be King of the Castle are smoothed away and because the grass is kept so short, nothing *but* grass can grow. Left rough, that grass would be interspersed with wild flowers. A few packets of seeds scattered randomly in spring would produce a bounteous crop of wild things which could be picked. Late in summer there would be standing hay to crawl about in . . .

Dogs by the hundred spend their owners' working days loose in this park. I am sorry for them but much sorrier for British children whose list of phobias is headed by dogs and whose crawling, rolling and running is so often interrupted by a meeting with turds. Dogs must relieve themselves but on the whole they choose to do so where others have gone before. Ash pits would actually attract the neglected ones as well as providing a legitimate place for responsible owners to take their pets. Perhaps we need higher licence fees, large automatic fines for fouling and dog wardens to enforce the new restrictions. I do not know *how* city dogs should be controlled but I do know that their interests clash with those of our children and that people should come first.

The park caters for children with a 'playground'. It is surfaced in concrete, roughened to be non-slip and apparently designed to ensure that every tumble draws blood from a knee. It contains the 'standard' playground equipment which leads to so many ghastly accidents each year all over the country. There is nothing in it which a child under five can manage alone nor is the place one where a pre-school child can possibly be safe unless an adult follows him everywhere, foreseeing the flying feet on the swings. There are many surfacing materials available now which could be used for playgrounds; they range from hard-wearing ryegrass to new kinds of synthetic rubber. There is a wide range of play-equipment, too, which could be installed for the very young, ranging from play-houses through sandpits to first-climbing frames. But given that councils already equip such places and staff them, it would cost no more to break right away from the conventional 'Playground' model and instead provide tree-stump stepping-stones, a boat-sailing pool, a few rabbits or guinea pigs, a mound of earth with steps up one side and a slide down the other, perhaps even a couple of giant inflatable cushions to jump and roll about on.

A little further on there is a paddling pool and here the authorities have proved their desire to protect very little children from 'big rough boys' by banning the fifteen inches of water to any male over the age of ten or female over fourteen. They have not apparently realized that if adults may not enter the water, small children cannot safely do so either. Water is blissful stuff and cheap, too. Provide such a pool by all means, but leave it to parents to choose quiet moments when bigger children are in school, or to help their very young ones come to terms with other members of the community. And why not some other kinds of water, too? A two-inch deep expanse would be both safe and glorious for toddlers and unlikely to attract much older children. Dig a 'river' and people could sail boats and leaves. Leave it open in winter and it is puddle-play in Wellington boots, or even sliding when it freezes. Site a sandpit nearby and you have made a beach and if one child insists on damming the stream this afternoon, another will take equal pleasure in shovelling the sand out again tomorrow.

Exceptionally, our park also has natural ponds, lakes really. One is the jealously-guarded preserve of fishermen who sit there grimly all week-end under umbrellas. Children are frowned upon although they do feed the ducks. I would put wooden platforms around the shallow edges so that they could fish too, with jam jars and shrimping nets and I would seed the water with frogspawn. The next pond is kept for noisy, expensive, remote-controlled boats but balsa wood and handkerchief sails are neither allowed nor catered for. Finally there are ponds for swimming but they are banned to children; 'We could not take the responsibility,' says the lifeguard grimly. 'But who is asking him to? A small child with his mother is *her* responsibility and natural water to paddle about in could be something local children remembered all their lives.

There are a lot of park-keepers and they expend much of their time and scarce patience on trying to stop children from doing things that they are going to do anyway. They would be far better occupied accepting, and facilitating, the inevitable. Bicycling, for example, is forbidden and continual. So where are the trike tracks? Where indeed is the mini-road system which could teach small children so much about road safety before they get hurt? Throwing balls against the walls of the various sports pavilions is forbidden too. Yet every time an older child starts school small brothers and sisters want to have a go at 'sevens' and every June we have Wimbledon in the making. Why not erect great wooden 'walls', close the fences where they would not show, and actually encourage children to use them? Everybody tries to climb trees and to swing from the low branches. They always have and they always will and the damage done cannot be compared to the ravages of the Elm beetle. But why not hang ropes from branches all over the park? Why not a few rope-ladders too? Lines of bollards are ideal for furtive leap-frog and I cannot imagine what harm that is supposed to do. There could be logs and stumps for leap-frog, for stepping-stones, for off-ground 'he' and just for sitting on, all over the place. There is a lot of concrete in the park and every now and again a school hopscotch craze produces wavery chalk squares which take us all back to childhood. Furious men with brooms come to sweep it away and to scold us for letting our four-year-olds vandalize public places. But rain washes away chalk and the ground is a glorious slate for the young. If adults do not want children's drawings on their ground, at least let them paint hopscotch pitches, paint mazes for children to thread their way around, paint roads for model cars and measured lines for long-jump practice . . .

But the real anger is displayed when young children try to use the park as if it were the real country which many of them seldom see. Anything which suggests a muddle is anathema to the keepers so a child making use of brushwood – which ought not to be there – or of piles of grass which are waiting to be removed, makes them see scarlet. 'Come out of there!' yelled one recently to a small boy who was making a 'wigwam' in some shrubbery undergrowth. 'Why?' he asked, 'I'm not hurting it . . .' 'That lot'll be cleared this week,' replied the park-keeper, 'and until it is you just keep away, understand?' He did not understand and neither do I.

Many of these ideas would be greeted with sympathy by members of parks departments if it were not for the question of safety and the bureaucrat's terror of being sued. I believe that the safety of pre-school children in their parents' care must start and finish with those parents and that pseudo-concern by the authorities is too often used as an excuse for doing nothing about anything. If a council erected stepping-stones or left piles of logs, a child might sprain his ankle and a rare, a very rare, parent might sue. But that same argument does not persuade the same council to take down the railings which might have been designed to castrate scramblers, nor to change the damaging surface of its playgrounds. You cannot make a park, a place for freedom, totally safe for children, you can only make it as satisfactory as possible in every way and then rely on parents both to shoulder their responsibilities and to be reasonable about the minor accidents which are part of a child's learning. Furthermore it is patently two-faced for a society which forces children to approach its parks through streets full of cars, to express concern lest they fall out of trees when they get there.

Many more ideas for children would be thought worth trying if the authorities were not so bitterly aware of vandalism. 'It

wouldn't be any use; it would be ruined/broken/stolen ...'
But while this concern again has some validity it is also again an
excuse for torpor. Fear of vandalism does not prevent people
from erecting bus shelters and telephone boxes, advertising
hoardings and sports pavilions. Adults want them so they are
put up. When they are vandalized, we curse and repair them.
The same should hold for facilities for the very young. At the
same time, most authorities would agree that vandalism is worst
where conditions are already sordid and life is boring. Clean,
bright, busy schools suffer less than the run-down Victorian
ones which throw out their pupils at four o'clock; the same
applies to blocks of flats and to parks and playgrounds. Adventure playgrounds, which are clearly seen to be genuinely *for* the
age-group responsible for most vandalism, suffer hardly at all.
So while the arrival of fifty rope-ladders might lead to an initial
burst of amazed treasure-taking, I do not believe that, once
everyone realized that there were always going to be rope-
ladders in the park, they would go on being pinched, slashed
and ruined.

Where else can a mother take small children at least for an
occasional treat or expedition? Well, if our streets are full of
them during the adult 'working day' our adult leisure facilities
are virtually empty except in the evenings and at week-ends.
Yet many of these, including rate-supported ones, have to stay
open, warm and staffed even when they have little adult custom.
Many of them could improve the value-for-money they get
from their capital plant and their wage-bill, as well as improving the quality of life of many families, if they would think
about providing for small children. Libraries have already been
mentioned and their possible scope is almost unlimited. Swimming pools are beginning to encourage mothers and babies and
some even heat their water an extra few degrees to cater for
them. But as long as pools are designed with a 'shallow' end of
two feet six inches, they will be of marginal use to toddlers who
want to go it alone but breathe at the same time. The bigger,
grander 'sports centres' appear convinced that their only daytime role is provision for schools. But any gymnasium, stadium,

squash or badminton court or roller-skating rink could be used by small children. What would they do there? Basically they would have a very large, covered, warm, safe space to play in. Anything else that happened would be up to the mothers . . .

Museum and art gallery staff are notoriously unwelcoming to the very young and, if challenged, express understandable fear of breakages. But their long, warm, carpeted galleries could provide hundreds of metres of toddling space for people who cannot possibly reach the display cases or the pictures and whose mothers would actually like to look while they walk. Why should excited young voices make these righteous guardians of our national heritage bristle so?

Cinemas and bingo halls have very restricted opening hours yet they exist, in most communities, complete with refreshment facilities, lavatories and adequate fire-precautions. I am not suggesting that three-year-olds should sit through movies or be taught to gamble, but I am suggesting that such places could be used by playgroups or community-groups or could simply open their doors once a week for sing-songs, puppet shows or story-telling.

A lot of towns, especially small ones, have special facilities which are expensive to maintain for occasional use and could also serve young children and their mothers. I can think, for example, of a number of covered markets which open only twice a week and are otherwise vast empty barns in which people could tricycle or simply run. I know several open markets, closed off from the streets and therefore not usable for car-parking, but complete with concrete sheep-pens and big auction sheds. They would be glorious places to play hide-and-seek, to climb and rush about. They could all be made into places to go, for fun.

If every mother with very young children had easy ways of making friends and obvious places to go in search of acquaintances, much of the outright loneliness which many experience would be lifted. If all those mothers came and went within a local environment which felt warm and accepting towards them and geared itself to their especial needs, getting out and about, alone or with those other mothers, would be both less of an effort and more worth whatever effort it cost. If there were also places to go to make a special point to a day or a week, to make the most of sunshine or to let off the steam that gathers when it rains, then daily life could begin to feel positively gay. A full-time mother leads a life which is under her own control and subject only to her programming. She can decide what she and her children will do today; she has no boss to set her chores or deadlines. At present many mothers do not enjoy this unique freedom in their working lives because their choice is between going drearily out or staying drearily in. Remove the drear of the local environment and going out into it would become a positive choice. In parallel, staying home would become a positive choice, too.

Home Conditions and Fun

Mothers and children do not want to be out or with others all the time. There is work to be done at home and there is also a need for them just to be together, in their own familiar surroundings, digesting, using and resting from the activities of the outside world. Happiness is a state of mind and can seldom be induced by material circumstances or objects. Nevertheless, as anyone who has tried rearing twins in one room with use-of-kitchen-and-bath will know, they can certainly help or hinder at the extremes. So while feeling good about being a mother and about society's view of the children she is mothering, will certainly help all mothers to make the most of whatever they have, a higher valuation by society should also bring about some changes in priorities. I do not want to get into the housing row here because the relative housing needs of a variety of groups within the population are both complex and well-known. But there is no doubt in my mind that a society which truly recognized the importance of new people and of the job their mothers do in bringing them up would also recognize that the best homes which are available at any particular time and place should go to these because they actually *use them most.* A mother does not spend the inside of five days in each week in a carefully-structured, warm, lit, ergonomically-arranged office or factory environment. She does not come home merely to eat and sleep and watch television. She and her children *live* at home. If there are any gardens available, it is the young families who should have them. If some families must live up in the sky, it should be those to whom a broken lift will present least problems, not those for whom it will mean imprisonment. Even within present homes there is a good deal which could be done and, in my view, should be done as of right, to improve a mother's working conditions. Many flats, for example, have balconies. But if you have a monkey-aged child that balcony is not a facility but a dangerous liability. It should be caged, 'roof' and all. Half a day's work would produce a place where children could play with messy materials and from which they could see the world. And it would take away a continual haunt from the mother who might have left the door open after hanging out the washing. Many flats are constructed around roofed galleries. Much could be cheaply done to make these wasted, and often sordid places into acceptable playspace. People own cars and their right to bring those vehicles to their own front doors is jealously guarded on most estates. Yet it is a right which conflicts with the right of young children to play outside *their* front doors. It is a question of priorities again.

Inside people's homes far more could be offered for the pleasure of mothers and young children through a variety of media. Radio and television, for example, present only a token number of programmes for this audience and are ruthless in rescheduling or cancelling them to suit the interests of other groups. 'Listen with Mother', for instance, has been recently moved from a slot just after most people's lunch to the late morning. Journalists have discussed this issue of timing, but nobody has discussed it with the mother-child consumers. The programme has been moved and if that means that many small people will miss it, too bad. Imagine the furore if Saturday afternoon's sport were shifted to the morning without consumer-consultation! Roughly half an hour's viewing-time is devoted each day to the under-fives by each television channel. But even this is cancelled with scarcely an apology should there be a live sporting event or state or political spectacle to show instead. The little that is offered is offered on sufferance.

One or two programmes for older children, and for schools, have shown the tremendous potential which these media have for enriching the lives of mothers and children listening, watching and participating together. A story told with pictures on television becomes a story for their private repertoire. It can be told again and again and perhaps a birthday can bring a book or a record or a tape ... Hearing traditional songs and nursery rhymes on the radio can recall to a mother the forgotten words to a tune she knows or the tune to which that particular rhyme goes. With hours devoted to reiterated pop music it seems extraordinary that no time at all is devoted to the music which is part of our children's heritage. There is scope for information, too. Most of the junk-material toys which are shown in the making are too difficult for most people: cardboard boxes and glue always end up as sticky cardboard boxes in my hands. But genuinely easy ideas for things to do and of ways to use everyday objects for fun can be grist to anybody's mill. Put the recipe for a dough which will not go mouldy on television and it will reach more mothers than it will ever reach through books on 'play'. And news: local radio stations preserve special slots for commuters, for air-travellers, for those in suicidal misery and for those seeking an evening's jazz. But where are the slots listing local 'happenings' for mothers and children?

Some of the most successful television programmes for older children are those which encourage participation and feedback, whether in collecting objects for charitable projects or in entering competitions and sending in pictures to the 'gallery'. Mothers and very young children could participate similarly. It would be fun to collect bottle tops with a three-year-old; fun to receive a thank-you letter and to see the collection growing in the studio; fun to see what was eventually done with the money. Programmes could send individual birthday wishes; play the records most toddlers' mothers said they enjoyed; show film of the animals voted 'most popular' or, even more interestingly, of those voted 'most feared' . . .

The radio phone-in format is comparatively new and extremely successful. There is tremendous scope within it for putting those mothers and children who wish it in touch with each other or with local groups. At present mothers can telephone the studio guest and, if the programme is aimed at mothers at all, he or she will be there to give them advice. But the studio could function equally well as a clearing-house *between mothers*. Through it mothers could swop equipment, find like-minded local friends and discuss the issues of their lives. Even the advice programmes might be more genuinely useful if they based themselves on their listener-participants. If I were trying to breast-feed twins, I would far rather talk to two or three other mothers who have done it, than to somebody like myself who has never had to try.

Newsprint could play a part, too. A few magazines run a 'children's corner' – usually the ill-designed Cinderella of the editorial material. But think of the thrill and the link between you and the adult world if mum's daily paper always had a picture for you to cut out and pin on your wall or a story for her to read to you or a puzzle for you to do. Children's comics raise many people's hackles. They do not raise mine as I believe that any form of pleasure-reading, for any age-group, is infinitely better than no reading at all and that reading 'tripe' is often the only first step towards 'good literature'. The fact that I am an inveterate reader of spy thrillers may have something to do with it. Anyway, where are the 'comics' for the very young to read with their mothers? Not everyone can afford children's books in quantity nor easily make frequent visits to a library. An illustrated story-paper at toddler and pre-school level would not be difficult to produce and could bring bedtime stories into the lives of children who do not get them now.

Toys, play-equipment and things to do have a large literature of their own; much of it excellent. But the mothers who buy these books tend to be those who are already aware that there are possibilities of which they may *not* be aware. Some of the space which women's magazines and women's pages currently allocate to knitting, sewing and improbable party-cooking could bring such things to a far wider audience if only editors believed that fun was as important as appearances.

None of these ideas would cost anyone (except possibly mothers) any money which is not already being spent. It is a reallocation of existing resources which I have suggested, not the investment of new ones. But with *more* money to spend, the possibilities are endless. Local authority libraries and arts committees accept that adults want to listen to music and to look at pictures, at home. Rate-supported libraries provide records and pictures on loan and we all, uncomplainingly, pay for them. Children want toys and equipment. If visiting toy libraries are put on my rates bill I shall not complain; will you? Charities, like the Red Cross, accept that when people are ill or disabled they need special equipment to make their lives easier and to give them pleasure. If you know who to ask you can borrow a wheelchair or arrange a regular supply of 'talking books'. Where are the 'talking books' for children who cannot yet read or the safety gates for crawlers with too many stairs? Young children in nursery schools get free use of educational consumables from drawing paper and felt-tip pens through clay to counting blocks. Where can a mother get these things for free if she chooses to keep her child at home rather than send him to the state?

Where we spend money on under-fives at all, we spend it on those who are away from their mothers, and on health care and advice for all. Money for fun, money for a way of life which can be more than just possible is reserved to different groups.

Instant Comfort and Instant Assistance

Being entirely responsible for the life and well-being of a small new person is an anxious business. Maybe it should not be. Maybe better preparation for parenthood, more information about the variegated strands of child development and more warm contacts with other parents would enable us all to stay calmer. But I doubt it. It is all very well to know, in theory, that a baby will eat when he is hungry. It is quite another to stay calm when, for the third meal running, your own child indicates that he is not. It is helpful to know that many children do not stand alone when they are one-year-old, but the knowledge does not quell the unease induced by an afternoon with a friend's one-year-old who walks around your own sitter. It is invaluable to know that expressions of hate are normal in three-year-olds, but the hate expressed by your own is of special intensity – isn't it?

True or apparent *medical* emergencies are well catered for by the National Health Service, through general practitioners and hospital casualty departments. But the anxiety-peaks which most parents suffer are not usually of this kind and they know that they are not. You cannot make an emergency call because a minor incident has brought latent anxiety suddenly to the surface.

Recognized long-term anxieties about health or development are usually dealt with sympathetically by well-baby clinics and health visitors who will offer as many appointments as a mother feels she needs. But appointments have to be made in advance and often a mother does not know on one Wednesday that she will want to talk again next Wednesday. Even if she sets herself up a regular series of appointments, they will probably prove impossible to keep. It seems idiotic to wake a baby from a peaceful nap in order to take him to the clinic to discuss his sleeplessness . . .

I believe that we need a drop-in service to which mothers can go as and when they feel the need and as and when they can manage it. Often what they need when they get there will be no more than a more fortunate woman might get from her own mother on a casual afternoon call. But the fact that she does not need much does not mean that she does not need it greatly, and now.

The best well-baby clinic I know does recognize this need and try to meet it. The regular sessions are held and, on different days, special clinics – antenatal, dental and so forth – are held there too. Around the edges, so to speak, the place is informally open to everybody. The toy-strewn waiting-room has a hot drinks machine and there are two receptionists who are extremely good at filling in forms. Mothers use it in many ways which were not strictly intended. Many come simply for the reassurance of its existence. A study of its use would be well worthwhile.

Along with instantly available comfort, instant assistance is needed too. Some mothers, at some stages in their child-rearing lives, live in a perpetual state of crisis, often largely due to the impossibility of going out without their children and the difficulty of going out with them. A mother may urgently need to get a prescription filled. She cannot take a sick baby with her to the chemist yet, if she waits until an older child or partner gets home, that chemist will be closed and the nearest open one may be miles away. She may have forgotten to buy potatoes on early closing day. She may have locked herself out and be unable to leave her children on the pavement while she burgles her own flat. She may be overtaken by a vomiting attack and literally unable, for a few hours, to keep the children safe amid dashes to the lavatory. She may simply have reached a point where she knows that, if somebody does not do something, she will throw her crying baby out of the nearest window. From potatoes to battering? Yes, that is very much the range of a mother's life.

Traditionally it was a parent's own mother who filled this vital role of general-helper-in-moments-of-need. Maybe one day it will be so again because a genuine choice of the role of parent may produce a change in grandparenting also. But in the immediate future own-mothers cannot be relied upon. Many of them are far away and those who are not are usually at work when a mother needs them most which is always *now*.

A first line of defence could be the telephone. The Post Office is making an embarrassing profit and its engineers are already installing free telephones in the homes of some who are old or handicapped. It is recognized that such people can cope with independent life better if they have a telephonic link with the

147

outside world for use in emergencies. I believe that every mother who is at home with small children is equally entitled to such a life-line. The possibility of giving telephones to some people who could pay for them themselves is far less awful than the actuality of not giving them to those who cannot. Being able to telephone would deal with many of the practical crises and it would help with the more emotional ones too. Experimental schemes for mothers, similar to those offered to despairing people by the Samaritans, show that mothers want and will use such a service. Phone-in radio programmes point the same way. A telephone also helps with that other intractable problem: transport. How do you get a choking child to hospital if you have no car? You telephone for an ambulance, if you have a telephone . . .

But more is needed. That grandmother was not just a service, she was a person too. Could one woman in every couple of streets not undertake to be available to any mother who cared to come or to telephone? Professional social workers will throw up their hands in horror. Such an 'unqualified' person might 'do harm'. Indeed she might if we see her as a caseworker. But she is filling the role of relative, friend or neighbour. She is guaranteeing only to be a friendly person who will not be out 'at work' when she is needed. Is it really so dreadful to think of this untrained person being faced with a schizophrenic mother and failing to recognize her psychosis through her misery? To me it is not dreadful to contemplate because at present that ill and unhappy mother may have nobody at all to talk to. And nobody is far less likely to help her than somebody who is, after all, a 'trained human being'.

Of course there are hazards to such an idea. Of course some such women would prove to be interfering or gossipy or to be using a helpful role for their own selfish ends. But the same is true of anybody; relation, neighbour or friend. The mothers who chose to involve themselves with this local aide would have to cope with her just as they would have to cope with any other person whom they met in any other way. But I do believe that the possible benefits would outweigh the problems. What do you say to a friend in difficulties when there is nothing immediate she needs of you? You say, 'You know I'll be there if you need me . . .' What do you want people to say to you when you have problems? The same message: 'Call if there is anything you want . . .' Those of us who have, and always have had, people who cared about us find it difficult, perhaps, to imagine what it is like to feel that there is nobody, anywhere nearby, who cares. Human beings are social and interdependent creatures and when the chips are down anybody is better than nobody and anything is better than isolation.

Another untapped source of practical help is our teenagers. As a society, we label these as a distinct group and then fear them. We fleece them as consumers but we do not repay them with respect. We keep them in schools with long 'holidays' yet we refuse them responsibility as young citizens and leave them with too little to do. Cautiously, some schools and playgroups begin to cooperate to the pleasure and benefit of all age-groups. Equally cautiously, some organizations begin to arrange visits by young people to the elderly and the housebound and it seems to work. In the United States, a high-school girl is the obvious babysitter and she benefits from the experience of sharing another family's life just as much as that family benefits from her services. I believe that many adolescents need, above all, to feel that they are useful and that they are trusted and I believe that they *are* needed and *could* be trusted to provide many kinds of help for mothers.

Fathers

If company, fun, help and comfort are some of the needs of people who are mothering, is not providing them part of the role of people who are being fathers? In an ideal world, yes. But in the real world of most families, no. I have left fathers on the sidelines of this book because that is where most fathers realistically find themselves during the early years of their children's lives. I am no advocate of society as it is; like many people I should like to see it change. But this book is a plea for mothers and until, or unless, society does change, their day-to-day needs cannot usually be met entirely within their partnerships.

Many men, far more than an outsider could deduce from our media, would like to take a full and equal part in the rearing of their children. But our society is based on wage-earning and on a strong accompanying work-ethic. Everybody has to work for a living from the time he or she finishes 'being educated' until compulsory retirement looms up forty to fifty years later. Society will not willingly spare even one member of a breeding pair from that labour market to rear the young. It certainly will not excuse both members of the pair to work together in partnership.

A very few families do manage to organize their lives so that the rigid distinctions between work-place and home, labour and leisure, are blurred, and the whole of life, including child-rearing, can become one. It can be so in farming, small-holding or market gardening. Work and play go on in the same place and at the same time. What is produced is used directly by the people who produce it, as well as being used to obtain money for the things other people produce. Children are born into an existing scheme of things and their advent does not bar their mother-person from participation, nor separate her from the life she was leading before. Their care can be shared between the parents in any way they choose, and, as the children grow, there is work in which they can participate and call it play.

To a lesser extent the same kindly mixture of lives can exist wherever a couple live 'over the shop' – whether it is a retailer's or a doctor's surgery – or wherever the work aspect of life is carried on from home, whether that means freelance journalism or plumbing. Where it is so, mothers are unlikely to be lonely, isolated or bored. But it can be so for only a minute proportion of families. In the vast majority, one member of the breeding couple has to go out to work to support the other and the young. The one who is out will usually be gone from something like 8 a.m. to 7 p.m. five or six days of forty-eight to fifty weeks each year. That person is, by definition, going to miss most of the waking hours of young children. And that person is almost always their father.

Within this reality, society's feelings about fathers are deeply entangled in the confusions of the women's movement and the aggressive male-bashing which too often accompanies or underlies its arguments. It is fashionable to exhort men to take a more active part in their young children's lives, but the exhortations seldom have even a pretended relevance to the needs either of the men or of the children. In essence they comprise a shrill insistence, by women for women, that men should 'do their share', backed by loud, female squeaks of 'unfair!' I do not believe that this is getting us anywhere we want to go. It is yet another version of the 'let mothers out' rather than 'help them through' attitude. 'Let *him* try taking care of the kids all day; let him see how *he* likes it . . .' Women have certainly been stereotyped for generations, but the male-stereotypes which are now bandied about are ultimately just as damaging to any hope of true sexual partnership. In an uncharacteristically obtuse article on 'fatherhood', a rightly-respected female journalist recently wrote:

> As for lecturing spotty boys in schools about the joys of fatherhood – well, I can already hear the sniggers likely to emanate from the nasty little beasts . . .

The boys I have 'lectured' were, on the whole, less spotty than their female peers and certainly no more sniggery. Some were already clear that they would one day want to reproduce themselves (as opposed to just having sex, you understand). Others were unsure. All were interested in discussing the subject. Several, at thirteen, made the point that if women were not so 'fucking bossy' about whether or not couples had children, men would get a chance to decide whether or not they wanted to be fathers and the ones who did want to 'might be fucking good at it'. So there.

I believe that the current pressures on fathers, as a class of male persons, are actually counter-productive for all concerned. Women talk as if men went out to work for fun; to escape domestic chores and to enjoy themselves in a male world, or one full of free and gorgeous non-mothers. The men, most of whom make long and exhausting journeys to boring and exhausting jobs purely in order to make money, understandably feel resentful. At home, they meet up with their partners and find them tired, harassed and depressed; so they have guilt to add to their anger. In a furious attempt to show that they will do what they can within the limits of their daily absence, they focus on the external chores of their wives' lives. I know men who get up at six every morning to do a share of the day's nappies and housework before going to their own jobs. Yet in a real partnership, would that hour not be more valuable spent in that bed – with a child or two added in on suitable occasions? I know other families in which whenever the father *is* at home, the mother is 'free to go out'. Like shift-workers, they 'man' their children and never, as a result, enjoy being together, either as a couple or as a family.

Some pressure is being put on the industrial and commercial world to reduce or break-up the working day so as to give fathers both more hours and more flexibility within which to share in child-care. Flexible working hours and job-sharing are both advocated. But at a time of high unemployment, why should employers put themselves out to accommodate parents? Of course I wish that they would, but I am quite unable to see any likelihood of them doing so. Of course it sounds logical to say that an office worker who is contracted to work for forty hours each week should be able to choose which hours of the day he will use for that contract. But in practice it is tiresome. Everybody else works from 9 to 5.30, and takes a lunch-hour from 12.30 to 1.30. Somebody who arrives at 7 a.m., works through lunch and leaves at 3.30, will be out of step. People who want to speak to him at 4 p.m. will not find him and he will be available,, or manning the telephone, during a lot of hours when his presence is not useful. In a factory situation it is even more difficult. Production lines and machines run for certain periods between maintenance and require specific periods for warming up and so forth. It is not entirely unthinking brutality which makes employers say 'no'.

One day all this may change. Some people believe that the electronic revolution will eventually out-date the concept of full-time work and its ethics altogether, just as the development of farming out-dated full-time hunter-gathering and the social organization which must have gone with that way of life. If that happens our main social problems may centre around leisure – around what people are to do with themselves when producing what they need no longer takes most of their time. Then, the rearing of a new generation of people might become relievedly involving for both partners and the child-care years a time people looked forward to just because it contained a real *raison d'être*. But unless or until that happens, attacking fathers for being unable to share full-time in the full-time job of mothering can only distort everybody's view of what both mothering *and* fathering are really about. The chores are not the point; the point is the people. To make a man think that he helps a mother to be a mother by doing the washing for her is to denigrate her role. To make him spend what little time he has cleaning up after his children, instead of talking to them, is to denigrate his.

If women who choose to be mothers, and their spokespeople, could accept that parenting is vitally important, that children need at least one parent around all the time, that mothers who fill this need are doing a proud job and that their working conditions are appalling and need improving within the community, I think fathers would gain a great sense of release. Instead of being screamed at to replace or release mothers, they would be being asked to be better fathers. Instead of being blamed for conditions which are not within their control, they would be being asked to help their partners to get them improved. Instead of being labelled 'irresponsible' for leaving their partners in day-to-day charge, they would be recognized as equally responsible for the overall, and especially the emotional, well-being of their families. Within that set of attitudes, men and women, who are increasingly learning to feel themselves as equals in the world outside child-care, could feel themselves truly equal within it, too. Each has an important full-time job and each can help the other when a job is in crisis.

A father can do night-duty with a sick child; a mother can stay up late to type an urgent report. But when crisis time is over, each reverts to his or her own job; neither expects to get it done by the other and the mutual time in between is for every member of the family to enjoy each other.

Fathers have the right to enjoy their children. At present being a father carries almost no privileges in the outside world because every campaigner who is at all concerned with the family is concerned to attack men on behalf of women. The interests of mothers and children and the cause of true sexual equality could all be better served by recognition of fatherhood as a role which many men have *and want* to fulfil. Campaign reasonably for what is feasible and employers and union leaders (many of whom are fathers as well as men) might actually facilitate the small changes which could alter the quality of many families' lives.

Paternity leave, for example, is a privilege which ought to be a right. Few men are going to have more than two or three children during their working lives. Two weeks for each baby adds up to only four or six extra weeks of paid leave in a forty-year span of employment. Some employers already give it. I believe that all could easily be persuaded to and that it would start many families off right.

Many men already take unpaid leave in times of family crisis. Others, luckier or less responsible, turn it into paid leave, with the help of a sick note. It should not be difficult to create an equitable system which recognized the fact that there are times in every family's life when a father ought to be able to be at home. Our doctors can already prescribe a large variety of foods and appliances, as well as medicines, to those who are ill. It would not be difficult to give them the authority to prescribe a partner's presence when called to a sick mother or a seriously-ill child.

In large firms and factories, holiday periods are often picked by lot or by seniority. If the needs of families were truly recognized, priority of choice would automatically be given to the men with young children. An older man may want to be off during Whitsun week, but do his wishes really weigh, in terms of human pleasure and pain, with those of the younger man who wants to be free to share a school half-term or playgroup break with his family? Over important holidays such as Christmas and Easter, work-forces are often drastically reduced. Surely the few men who must work should be picked from among the childless? If anyone can be at home on Christmas morning surely it should be the fathers with stockings to open with small people? Of course other people would grumble: 'Why should he get special treatment just because he's got kids . . .?' Because those kids matter and because he matters to them, that's why.

Shift-work is already used, by some men, to facilitate their family lives. When I worked with families newly-delivered of twins, for example, many of the fathers got themselves put on to night-shifts because their partners really *could not* cope with two new babies as well as an existing toddler . . . But the needs of all fathers and small children could be built into our shift work planning if their rights were recognized. A midday to midnight stint, for example, can prevent a father from seeing his children at all, if they happen to be at playgroup or at school when he gets up in the middle of the morning.

But it is in the area of overtime that the most radical re-think should be carried out. At present, in many jobs, the 'basic wage' and the 'working week' bear no relationship either to the hours a man is expected to work or to the pay he expects to earn. Unions negotiate for shorter hours so that more hours are left to be paid at overtime rates. The actual hours that most men work are rising, despite the fall on paper. Men with young children are the ones who most need to earn extra money, as well as being the ones who most need time at home. If the vociferous women's movement campaigners, who have proved so successful in catching public attention and bringing about changes, would concentrate on that basic anomaly, we might get somewhere.

Children come in two sexually-different models and they need two sexually-differentiated parents. I can already hear the

155

screams of rage that statement will provoke, because it carries images of little girls copying mummy in doing the housework while brothers get nice and dirty with dad, mending the car. But sex is far more basic than the stereotyped behaviours our society has attached to it. If a truly unisex society is really on the way, something extremely odd is going to have to happen to biology, and to related physiology and psychology, if it is to survive to prove itself. In the meantime sex differences exist; they are vitally important in their still ill-understood impact on human development and personality, and trying to be, or pretending that we are, all the same, is not helping us to understand more. But we do know that fathers are not mothers. And we can surely see, if we let ourselves look, that expecting them to fill the roles of pseudo- or apprentice-mother can only detract from their real roles as fathers and thus further deprive them and their children and the women-who-are-mothers, too.

Part-time Jobs

Most women who have small children stay at home to care for them. The bulk of this book has been devoted to the proposition that their lives, and those of their children, could be infinitely more satisfactory; so satisfactory, indeed, that some mothers who are currently working would elect to join them in full-time child-care, if the particular needs of women-who-are-mothering were recognized and met by society and its communities.

But while I do believe that creative caring for a child should be the central activity for whoever is doing the caring, this does not mean that I believe mothers should be excluded from the outside world; and that includes the world of work. Unlike certain Tory opposition spokespeople, who imply that the slogan 'children need their mothers' is a legitimate lever for forcing mothers out of the labour market to the benefit of currently unemployed men, I believe that work outside the home which can be carried on without disrupting the young children in it, is *one of the needs* of some mothers.

At present few employers are sufficiently in tune with the needs of young children or their mothers to consider the nature of the ideal outside job, much less to offer it. But possibilities do exist and should be exploited. The long-term attitude-change which I hope will one day produce a society which cares about children, will affect employers along with everyone else. But right now, tax and insurance inducements could be offered to employers to motivate them towards employing mothers. Such inducements are already offered to those who employ members of other social groups with special needs.

If a baby or young child is to experience his days and his relationships as a smooth continuum, a comfortable outside job for his mother must have very short hours. If the hours she spends away from him are to be valuable to the mother, they must almost all be spent 'on the job' rather than in travelling. So the comfortable job is local. Where can we find or create such jobs? At present many mothers who are officially classified as 'working' do have jobs that fit these criteria, but they are mostly within an extremely limited range. The mothers who work for twelve hours or less each week tend to undertake relief and rush-period work in local shops and service industries. A few work for others like themselves in settings where their children are also welcome: in playgrounds and so forth. A handful more use academic qualifications to enable them to teach a weekly seminar or lecture-course . . .

I believe that this narrow range of choices could be widely extended if it were recognized that wherever help is needed for just a few regular weekly hours, a qualified mother, living nearby, is the obvious person to provide it.

In the country town I know best, doctors, vets, auctioneers and a bank manager all hold twice-weekly sessions as the population does not justify full-time service. These 'sub-stations' are run by staff who are dragged, often reluctantly, up to twenty miles from the various headquarters. Yet each of these 'sub-station' sessions could provide a job for a mother living in that little town. And, given the saving in travel and overtime costs, the employers would not even lose significantly.

Who Cares?

Many small businesses and freelance workers require various kinds of help for a few hours each week. Although the bulk of the work is secretarial, there are also opportunities in a range of other skills from accounting, through developing and printing to electrical repairs. At present these needs are largely met by 'temps' who make up a full week's work by doing a few hours each for several employers. By definition these 'temps' are in a position to take full-time jobs instead. The hours they would release would again make brief jobs for mothers living close by.

Specialist teachers often work on a peripatetic basis, serving several, often widely scattered schools, each of which is entitled to only a few weekly hours of their time. Each such school could provide a comfortable job for a local mother who happened to be qualified. The present incumbents could devote themselves to areas where there are no such mothers, or to full-time, static employment. It is worth remembering that wherever this happened, professional time and public money would be saved on travel.

Sessional work is already highly developed in some professions and could develop further in more. A doctor can serve a practice well by taking two surgeries each week. It is difficult to see why other professionals cannot be helped to give whatever time they want to spare from child-care to their chosen outside jobs. Why, for example, would it be impossible for a solicitor to work for one day each week? People who particularly want to see Ms Jones know that they must make an appointment for a Thursday. People who just want to see a solicitor can see whoever is working today. Take the idea to extremes and you have job-sharing, and why not? It is only convention which demands that a professional office have full-time staff with a desk each ... Many such offices might be livelier and less back-biting places if more people were involved, and one can have a private and personal filing-cabinet without an exclusive desk.

Clearly there are many types of job which cannot be done on this basis. No production line could run this way and no long-term project, whether it was the building of a housing estate or the running of an institution, would fare well if each day brought a different personality to bear. But any job which naturally falls into separate segments, tasks or clients, can run, and run well, in this way.

Training, Re-training and Staying in Touch

Sensible women who are mothers recognize the fact that a chosen and total involvement in child-care does not last forever. While it may be many years before her children's needs become totally irrelevant to a mother's daily life, the school years bring a slowly-increasing independence which, ideally, is mutual. It is almost as sad to be a ten-year-old who feels he should stay at home after school in case his *mother* is lonely as to be a six-year-old who does not like to be at home after school because *he* is lonely.

While the desirability of courses for 'mature women' is beginning to be widely recognized, actual course-organization seldom recognizes the practical needs of those women who still have very young families, but who wish to prepare themselves for the future. There are courses in a vast range of subjects, available in increasing numbers of adult education colleges of one kind and another. But their lectures and seminars tend to begin at 7 p.m. which every mother knows to be both a busy and a vital point in most children's days. By 8.30 p.m. many mothers could leave sleeping children with partners or babysitters and attend without stress.

The Open University is a breakthrough and, with a very little adaptation, its courses could become relevant to many more mothers. Few, perhaps, have the habit of academic study or the peaceful circumstances in which to carry it out at home. But the idea of local study-groups, with local tutors, is built in to many Open University courses. Such a study group could be the mother-and-child group-with-a-purpose discussed earlier.

Many home study courses, using books, records, tapes and even simple 'teaching machines', are advertised commercially.

159

They too could be used by small groups of mothers, willing to support each other when motivation flagged and to facilitate each other when child-responsibilities became temporarily overwhelming.

Many women re-enter the world of full-time work only to find that the years they have spent growing up with their children count for nothing in the eyes of employers with younger, newly-qualified staff to choose among. I believe that, as well as facilitating women in acquiring new training and skills while they are mothering, we ought also to make it easier for them to keep up established ones. A freelance professional can charge relevant books and journals against tax: why cannot a mother? Local authority employees can charge up the costs of attending refresher courses: why not mothers? A student can have membership of restricted libraries and reduced subscriptions to journals, professional organizations and conferences. Why are not the same facilities available to mothers who were students once and are now in an even worse financial position than they were then? Given that ours is a society which places such high value on external, examination-type evidence of accomplishment, perhaps we even need a system through which a woman who had kept her pre-mothering skills in good order could prove that she had done so. If she could wave a recognized piece of paper, perhaps the computer firm or the laboratory would not be so quick to assume that she, aged forty, knew nothing of their technological advances in the past eight years. If she could show her six-monthly typing-speeds to the office manager, perhaps he would not pass her over in favour of that eighteen-year-old.

Day-care for Working Mothers

There will always be some mothers who want and/or need to hold down outside jobs while their children are very small. Some may enter mothering as a genuinely free and informed choice, yet still discover that it was the wrong choice for them.

Others may have jobs which they cannot bear to abandon altogether, even for a few years, and within which the minimal part-time work which they could do without disrupting their child-care is either impossible or not on offer. Yet others may find even adequate financial help less than they can earn outside, or simply feel that even given social facilities and status, they can still lead more satisfying lives as working mothers. So we shall always need some day-care. The question is: what kind?

I believe that for children under three there should be no form of socially approved *group*-care. My ideal society has no day nurseries, residential nurseries or creches in it. None at all. Babies and very small children each need a 'special' and continuous person or people and they need to have their daily lives based on somewhere they know as 'home'. So, for this youngest age-group, we have to think about mother-substitutes, either in the child's own home or in the caretaker's, which the child will come to know as partly his.

Socially-advantaged women have employed self-replacements for generations, in the form of nannies, who lived in the house and undertook the full-time care of the children whenever their mother wanted to do anything else. Britain is still said to train the best nannies in the world, but most of them are part of the export business now, lending status to homes in America and the Middle East rather than here. Few British families, even where the mother has very high earning-potential, can afford a nanny for the simple reason that having one usually means having domestic servants as well in order to make it clear to the nanny that she is not a servant herself . . .

Some working mothers try to replace themselves with au pair girls from other countries. Certainly having an au pair living in the house can enable a mother with older children to do a part-time job with equanimity and justice. But with under-threes and/or a full-time job, somebody will be being abused. An au pair is supposed to do a few hours of light work each day in return for pocket money, her keep and a share in family life and spoken English. Leaving her all day is against regulations and not what one would want for one's own daughter, temporarily resident in somebody else's home abroad. Leaving a baby or toddler, even for shorter hours, with a teenager who may, or may not, speak the child's language and/or have the least interest in him is fair to no one. How 'good' would you have been with a strange two-year-old with measles when you were seventeen and first away from home? Of course it *can* work because some au pairs, being people, *are* interested in small children, loving and lovable. But even when it does work it is not an ideal solution because the paragon will depart and the child will be desolate. She may be 'special' but she stops short of being 'continuous'.

Resident 'mother's help' is a newish title, coined to cover the employee who is willing to be both nanny and domestic help in one. Ironically, the going-rate quoted by an agency will be less than for a 'proper nanny', even though the employee will do so much more work. If the house is big enough to accommodate her without incurring an extra rent or mortgage charge and if the household bills are already so large that her 'keep' is camouflaged, a family may feel that it can afford one. But finding one is another matter. Few people will take it on unless the employer is offering something for which they have a great personal need; such as the facilities for their own child to be with them. Once again it can work, but it is very much more difficult than most people think to meet the needs of all the children concerned and to strike acceptable balances between such things as privacy and company.

The whole concept of resident service, whatever you call it, really belongs to an era when solitary women could neither find 'respectable' jobs nor, 'suitably', live alone. 'Living-in' provided much more than a wage; it provided a safe, secure and socially acceptable way of life. Now, single women do not need that security and protection. It seldom seems like an acceptable exchange for the loss of personal autonomy arising from living in somebody else's household.

But there are still two ways in which a woman who wants to go out to work may be able to get her child properly cared for in his own home. The first involves not service, but sharing. If two families – often, but not necessarily, single-parent families – discover that one mother wants to stay at home with her children while the other wants to go out to work, a shared house may solve all their problems. I know one in which the income earned by the working mother is equally shared with the child-caring one. I know another in which the working mother's children are of school age and the others are much younger. That mother is paid an agreed 'wage' for her after-school, holiday and emergency care. Obviously there are enormous potential difficulties in such an arrangement but there are also enormous potential advantages. It may be that the building of this sort of 'extended family' of contemporaries will prove the best escape from the restrictions we impose upon ourselves by cutting off the blood-families from which we came.

The problems of employing somebody who is resident and those likely to be involved in sharing a house can both be avoided if arrangements are made with a *daily* mother's help. A woman whose own children have started school but who still wants to be available to them after school and in the holidays will often welcome such work. The employing mother can go out to work part-time, leaving her child in experienced hands. The mother she is employing can also be out of her own home part-time without her children suffering. The two women genuinely provide for each other's needs and each has a part in ensuring the well-being of all the children involved.

Socially less-advantaged women have also been arranging individual care for their young children for generations, using baby-minders. I believe that the registration and increasing recognition of day-minders is one of the major social advances of the past few years and it is fascinating to watch professional and middle-class women leaping on to what was traditionally a working-class wagon. When day-minding first hit the headlines it was with opprobrium. Reference was made to baby-farms, and pathetic infants were depicted huddled into empty rooms, with nothing to do and only minimal care. But similarly dreadful pictures could all too easily be found among children living

163

with their natural parents or in institutional care. Children are vulnerable and there will always be some who will exploit them. Overall I see day-minding as the pattern for the future, wherever a child requires non-residential substitute-mothering outside his own home. It is an idea with many built-in advantages.

A woman who becomes a child-minder is almost invariably someone who has a baby or young child of her own and who wants to stay at home to care for him or her. This implies that she both recognizes her importance to her child and feels his importance to her. She is therefore likely to be sensitive both to the importance of other mothers to their children and to the feelings of mothers who face leaving children while they go elsewhere.

A child-minder's care is essentially individual for each child. Even if she looks after two or three children, they will not all be the same age. They will neither constitute, nor be handled as, a group, but rather as a family.

Like any other family, the children are cared for in their mother-person's home. The experiences they have, day by day, are home-experiences in a home-setting. They will not be offered tiny little lavatories just for them, as they would in a day nursery. But the lavatories they will use will be part of real life. All floors will not be covered with washable materials and washed by domestic staff, so there will be restrictions and limits on their activities just as there are in any home. But the kitchen, in which they suddenly 'help' to cook buns for tea on a wet afternoon, will be a real kitchen, and the treat-tea will be for the minder as well as for them. Just as mothers have other things to do beside watching and playing with their children, so the minder will sometimes be busy, too. The children are spared that combination of adult over-attention and adult boredom which is typical in settings where there are no grown-up activities except child-care.

Day-minders are not professional child-care workers so the care which they offer to children does not exclude the natural parents nor lower their self-esteem. Of course any individual minder may have strong views on particular aspects of child-rearing, but where these are at variance with the parents', they can be discussed between equals rather than between 'expert' and 'client'. Usually any real stumbling blocks are discovered early in the relationship and, if they cannot be sorted out, the child is moved. One couple, for example, had to try three minders before they found one who shared their horror at the very idea of a smacked hand or bottom. But once they had found one, they knew that her views would hold because they were the views of an individual person, not the policy of an institution, or the opinions of a staff member who might be away on holiday next week. Another family found a minder whose only 'snag' was that she gave their baby a dummy. Those parents were able to accept the little girl's obvious contentment as a demonstration of the loving care she was receiving. They decided that being 'anti-dummies' was less important than being pro-happiness.

The minder's lack of professionalism leaves her free of any obligation to try to be objective about the children for whom she cares. She can and will become emotionally involved with them because she takes them into her own home and family. While of course the relationship between a minder and a child can go wrong (just as it can go wrong between a mother and her child), it will at least have human depth and complexity. Young nursery nurses, who weep for the children they must leave in the course of their training, are told again and again not to involve themselves. Eventually they learn, in self-preservation, not to mind too much about any one child. Yet minding is the essence of good minding. Of course a minder's emotional involvement can lead to jealousy between her and the child's parents. But a child's capacity to love more than one person usually kills the jealousy and leaves the love; and it is the love that he needs.

Because the minder is an ordinary mother living in an ordinary home in her own community, the child for whom she cares remains part of that community and able to benefit from whatever it can offer. Children in nurseries tend to be isolated within them and exposed only to what they contain. But the child who is minded by Mrs Jones goes where she goes. He goes shopping or to the park; he meets her friends and/or his own; he 'helps' her with her window-boxes or her cats and together they can use the local playground or join the playgroup. Often the minder's home will be close to the child's, so that the community he explores will be the same whichever of his 'special' people has charge of him. A nursery, on the other hand, is likely to draw children from a wide area so that the two major aspects of his life are geographically separate as well as being separated in every other way.

Where a successful relationship is forged between mother, minder and child, it can have both continuity and flexibility. The continuity can, and often does, span the child's life from infancy, through going to playgroup with his minder, to returning to her at tea-time and in the holidays once he starts school. Of course this does not always happen. A minder may herself wish to give up child-care in favour of a job outside her home, once her own children reach a particular age. But at least the possibility is there. A child whose infant-care is put in the hands of a day nursery will not get the chance to go to playgroup and will have to face a completely new caretaking situation in the holidays, as soon as he is of school-age. Flexibility is important too. Minders try, in self-protection, to be strict about mother's timekeeping. They do not want to be left with a tired toddler on their hands when they are supposed to be bathing their own children and preparing for the evening with their families. But because they are in their own homes, minders do not 'close'. The working mother whose train breaks down, whose watch stops or whose boss lays her job on the final line of an urgent report, knows that her child will be all right. She may face an irate minder but she will not face disaster. Perhaps only mothers who have lived through this situation can fully understand the clock-watching stress that is involved. Being relieved of the worst of it is a big factor in favour of minders. But the flexibility works the other way, too. Once a child is swallowed up into his day at a nursery, it takes a brave parent to remove him before the proper time. But because she is at home and doing her own thing, no minder is going to object to a mother collecting her child early if she happens to find herself free.

I should like to see every baby or small child who cannot have full-time care within his own family, offered the balance in somebody else's. That would mean more, many more, day-minders than we have at present. But I do not only see the day-minding system as relevant to the under-threes. I also see it as the solution to the problems of mothers whose children are old enough to benefit from two or three hours each day at a nursery school, a playgroup or in a nursery class, but whose jobs span longer hours than does that benefit. Where the government would like to see the hours and the functions of all facilities for the threes to fives extended, to provide day-care as well as group-experience, I find this idea abhorrent. The activities of a good pre-school group are predicated on a two to three hour attendance. The short attention span, tenuous social control, sensitivity to noise and general over-stimulation of these very young children make it impossible to run a valuable group for much longer at a time. Terminate the 'activities' and call the rest of the day 'care', and you undo, during the afternoon, the creative work of the morning. Children need to go *home*; to rest and recuperate; to think through and play out the things they have experienced within the group. It stands to reason that they cannot do this while they are still in that group. So, if their own homes are not available to them, I should like to see such children going to minders' homes. And, in an ideal world, these would be the same, familiar, second-homes in which they had received day-care through their earlier years.

A campaign to recruit more day-minders seems the obvious solution and such campaigns are already running in some parts of the country. But they must proceed with unusual delicacy if laudable attempts to make minding better are not to spoil what it already can be. We need local authority recruitment. We need registration of minders' both to avoid abuses and to disseminate information about who has vacancies. But we must, at all costs, avoid turning minding into a local authority service because if we do that we shall set minders apart from the mothers and children they serve and turn them into yet another bunch of alienating experts. We have to ensure that children are cared for in reasonable conditions, yet we have to avoid setting arbitrary standards which will prevent warm, loving women with ordinary homes from extending care from their own children to those of another mother. We have to see to it that minders are paid at rates which make the job worthwhile and make it possible for them to provide adequate meals, enough warmth, play materials and the small treats that differentiate one day from the next. But if we lay down 'wage-scales', we risk driving some mothers to the unregistered minder or introducing means-tested local authority grants which will inevitably make the service the authority's direct responsibility.

There are no easy answers to these problems but remembering who day-minders are, and why they are willing to mind other people's children, will help us to avoid some pitfalls. The ideal minder is somebody who has a child of her own and wants to stay home-based for his or her sake. The child may be a baby, a pre-school child who is out in the mornings, or a school-child who is at home only at teatime and in the holidays. But the minding-mother's basic aim is to *be there for him*. She therefore has strong personal reasons for doing the job which, to some extent, make the comparability of her wages for minding with the wages she could get in an outside job irrelevant. If she were not minding she probably would not be working at all. If she were working, she is conscious of the stress it would cause to her and to her child. This theoretical minder likes, and is interested in, children. If this were not so she would be among those who do seek jobs outside their homes rather than among those who seek ways to stay there. The home which she has is suitable for children to be in, at least to the extent of being good enough for her own. Her knowledge and skills with small people have similarly been adequate for her own family. She is, therefore, truly a substitute-mother and one with a proven track-record. She may, of course, be a vicious woman; a secret batterer of children; a sadist seeking new victims. She may be an avaricious and unthinking person who believes that she can make money out of the desperation of mothers who want to work. She may be, but the possibilities are remote and can easily be guarded against by a simple registration procedure. It is what comes after registration which endangers the very ordinariness which makes her a good mother-substitute. Too much emphasis on the number of available lavatories and the size of her rooms means that the authorities are setting standards for minded children which are different from those which are accepted at home. And this is counter-productive because 'at home' is what we want him to be. Too much enthusiasm in facilitating home improvement grants for would-be minders and the authorities risk encouraging minders to take several children at a time rather than just one or two. Taken to extremes, this approach would undo the whole point of minding by making it into group, rather than individual, care. Too many training courses and the authority risks making minders see their charges as challenges, rather than as people.

I believe that society could help day-minders, the children they care for and the parents who trust them, by exactly the same means which I have been proposing for blood-mothers and their offspring. In south London, one or two boroughs have already instituted, for minders alone, several of the 'services' I have been putting forward for mothers. Registered minders have telephones and they have a telephone number on the end of which is a social worker with a car, ready to help in any emergency from taking an ill child to the doctor, to taking over the household if the minder is suddenly laid low with a migraine. They have a minder-and-children's club. They have a permanent welcome in the local playgroup. They have a mobile toy library which calls regularly. They have each other's addresses, support and company and, judging by the groups to whom I have spoken, they *and* the children have full and enjoyable lives. Yet they remain perfectly ordinary women in the homes which are ordinary for their districts. They are true mother-substitutes for babies and children whose mothers do not want to be there all the time. So if we provided community facilities, help and acceptance for *all* mothering-people and their charges, we should facilitate day-minding as well as mother-care. The less we see minders as a separate group the better, because one child's mother is another child's minder and vice versa.

Coda

A confluence of social rivers is building up a dangerous tide. The river of work makes us see ourselves in terms of the jobs we do for money; it assigns us both external status and self respect relative to what we earn to spend on the things we produce. The economic river must flow faster and faster to maintain the growth economy on which it depends, so it sucks in more people to produce and consume more. The rip-race of the women's movement pours in to get a share for women – as a group – of all that there is for men – as a separate group. And we are all carried along, swimming, dog-paddling or floating with the current, but always in the same direction.

The tide throws up increasing numbers of casualties and for them we build a growing complex of canals into which they can be hauled by the helping professions which will tow them through the system and launch them again, into that river.

Among those casualties are all new people and their mothers. Human beings cannot give birth and nurture young in deep, fast-flowing water. So anyone who has a child must scramble out of the mainstream and into the hands of the professionals. There she finds herself in the semi-stagnant canal-water and it is in this second-best environment that she must try to mother her baby. She may be fortunate enough to find herself a pleasant backwater where she is not too painfully conscious of the main tide of society passing her by. But it will suck at her. Soon she will be encouraged to leave her child, who still cannot swim, in the hands of those professionals, in order to be free to dive back in.

I believe that this tide must be diverted, that it must be flattened out so that society laps a quieter, wider shore with many choices of direction. We have let the tide build up, but that does not mean that we are committed to travelling with it, leaving our future people stranded. There are no laws governing human decision-making. Within wide limits we can choose what kind of society we want to have and it is still open to us to make one which is for people to manage and enjoy.

In order to try and show the enormously humanizing effects which tiny tidal diversions might have, I have touched on many complex and wide-ranging issues – such as national economics and trades union policy – and I have specified minutiae ranging from town planning, through retailing to municipal gardening. Each and every one of these is a specialist area and in daring to write about it I have laid myself wide open to the experts who know so much more than I do. Of course many will criticize. But I hope that some experts who are struck by the undoubted inadequacy of my lay-ideas will react more positively by putting forward their own. If streets cannot be made safer and more suitable for small human beings in the ways that I have suggested, how can it be done? If professionals cannot undertake to act as go-betweens for new mothers, how can they be put in touch? The one thing that is certain is that all these things can be done, somehow, if enough people want them done.

We could make a society in which people cared enough about people to realize the primacy of new people.

We could make that a society in which those who chose to produce new people knew what being parents must involve.

We could ensure that the job those self-selected parents did was recognized and rewarded with a place at the top of our status hierarchy and our priorities' list.

We could teach everyone to recognize that inconvenience or unhappiness in the lives of parents reflects badly on their children who will be parents themselves next time around, and we could train professionals to devote themselves to helping parents through, rather than out of, the early years of child-care.

We could recognize that while child-care is for parents, parent-care is for everyone.

It could all happen. As a society of self-determining, inter-linked human beings, we have the power to make it happen. But it will only happen if we believe that babies' and small children's development depends on their happiness and that their happiness depends on their 'special' adults. And if we believe that their development and happiness matters. And if we care.

References

A SELECTION OF REPORTS, ARTICLES AND BOOKS
RELEVANT TO THIS ARGUMENT

Services for young children with working mothers, Central Policy Review Staff, HMSO (1978)

The family in society, 'Preparation for Parenthood', Department of Health and Social Security, HMSO (1974)

Good enough parenting, Central Council for Education and Training in Social Work, HMSO (1978)

Women in Britain, Central Office of Information Reference Pamphlet 67, HMSO (1975)

The needs of the under-fives, National Union of Teachers, Hamilton House, Mabledon Place, London WC1 (1977)

Nursery education and playgroups, National Association of Head Teachers, Maxwelton House, 41–3 Boltro Road, Hayward's Heath, Sussex (1978)

Under fives, Trades Union Congress Publications Department, Congress House, Great Russell Street, London WC1 (1978)

I want to work but what about the kids?, Equal Opportunities Commission, Summary of:
   Day care for school-age children, Robin Simpson (1978)
   A survey of childcare for pre-school children with working parents: costs and organisation, Peter Mottershead (1978)
   Alternative models of group childcare for pre-school children with working parents, Peter Moss (1978)
   All available from The Equal Opportunities Commission, Overseas House, Quay Street, Manchester

The cycle of deprivation, Rt Hon. Sir Keith Joseph, PPA Publications (rev. 1975)

Facts and figures 1977, PPA Publications (1978)

Mother and toddler groups – a basis for discussion, PPA Publications (1977)
   All available from The Pre-School Playgroups Association, Alford House, Aveline Street, London SE 11

Who Cares?

What shall we do with the under-threes?, Penelope Leach (January 1978)

The care of young children, Mia Kellmer-Pringle (June 1978)

    Both available from *Contact*, the magazine of the Pre-School Playgroups Association, 1 The Outgang, Heslington, York

Alternatives in pre-school provision, Willem van der Eyken (1977–8 series)

    Available from *Where*, the magazine of the Advisory Centre for Education, 18 Victoria Park Square, Bethnal Green, London E2

Women Wendy Collins, Ellen Friedman, Agnes Pivot, Wildwood House (1978)

Mothers: their power and influence, Ann Dally, Weidenfeld & Nicolson (1978)

Babyhood, Penelope Leach, Penguin Books (1975)

The needs of children, Mia Kellmer-Pringle, Hutchinson (1978)